'The book reminds us of Jesus C ⸻
A Christ-centred servant leader ⸻⸻⸻ ⸻ ⸻⸻⸻⸻ ⸻⸻⸻,
and focuses primarily on the growth and well-being of
people.' – **Rev Dr Siegfried Ngubane**, Director, SIM SA

'Tim's message is relevant and enriching for leaders
today, from all walks of life, whether in Christian
ministry or in business.' – **Charmaine Groves**, Executive
Chairman, South African Business Resources Institute

'*Grab A Towel* cuts to the heart of Christ-centred
servant leadership. It's packed with truth and rich experience – a must-read for those seeking practical tools
on how to stick it out and lead in a manner counter to
the overwhelming culture of the day.' – **Susannah Farr**,
CEO, Gold Youth Development Agency

'When I read the words, "moving people onto God's
agenda" I knew this was going to challenge me to the core
and I was right. Get ready for adjustment after adjustment because that's what this book is all about. Grab
a towel and enjoy the journey.' – **Anthony Liebenberg**,
Senior Pastor, Life Church, Cape Town

PRAISE FOR *GRAB A TOWEL*

'Tim has modelled the leadership style he sets out so clearly in this book, even in extremely challenging times. The leadership skills and examples here will assist leaders in any organisation or business to follow the most successful leader of all time, Jesus Christ.' – **Stefan van der Walt,** Founder and Chairman, Premium Group and Premium Dolberg Group of Companies, and Founder and Chairman, ADDLIFE Foundation

'In *Grab A Towel*, Tim Tucker presents a practical, honest look at leadership and encourages us to look back over our shoulder and see who is following us. Tim shares of personal failures and successes, and every account is based on authentic lived experiences.' – **Graham Power,** Founder, Global Day of Prayer and Unashamedly Ethical

'I've worked closely with Tim over the last few years and recognise him as an outstanding leader from whom we have much to learn. This dynamic and powerful material is essential reading for any leader who wants to go the distance.' – **Andy Hawthorne OBE**, Founder and CEO, The Message Trust

'The teaching in Tim's book really lives up to the title. It is packed with leadership experience and truth from a practitioner, not just a speaker.' – **Paul Hallam**, Founder and Lead Pastor, The Lighthouse, Manchester UK

'I pray that *Grab A Towel* will refocus the lives and ministries of both established and emerging leaders. Written with thoughtful biblical insight and from rich experience, Tim brings a timely reminder of who and how we are called to follow. Excellent!' – **Gareth Lloyd-Jones**, Senior Pastor, Ridgeway Community Church (South Oxfordshire) and Team Leader, Life in the Spirit Network

'Why *Grab A Towel*? Having worked with thousands of churches around the globe, I believe the value of Christ-centred servant leadership is beyond description. Yet, Tucker does it and does it well, because he has caught what can't be taught.' – **Dr Kent R. Hunter**, Founder of Church Doctor Ministries and author of *Who Broke My Church? 7 Proven Strategies for Renewal and Revival*

GRAB A TOWEL

GRAB A TOWEL

CHRIST-CENTRED SERVANT LEADERSHIP FOR THE 21ST CENTURY

TIM TUCKER

*the*message

First published in Great Britain in 2018 by The Message Trust
Lancaster House, Harper Road
Manchester, M22 4RG, UK

ISBN 978-1-9999036-2-6
eISBN 978-1-9999036-3-3

Cover design and typesetting: Simon Baker

To Mark
Mates on mission for twenty years

CONTENTS

FOREWORD

I have known Tim Tucker for a number of years now, and one of the attributes I really appreciate about him is that he has a servant's heart. I think that's why he is so successful, especially with young people. He doesn't talk so much, he is more of a doer of the Word – and as the title of this book indicates, the Christian walk is all about a servant's heart. I am greatly privileged to be his friend and especially to be there for him, even if it was from a distance, when he lost his dear wife not so long ago. The way in which he handled it really amazed me.

As you read this book, I think you will understand that it is about the 'upside-down gospel', so to speak. The San Bushmen of Southern Africa call the baobab tree the 'upside-down tree', because when it loses its leaves it looks like the roots are sticking in the sky and the tree is underground. Jesus said, 'if you want to be first in the kingdom of God you've got to be the last' (Matt. 20:26), and '...unless a grain of wheat falls into the ground and dies, it remains alone; but if it dies, it produces much grain.' (John 12:24).

As Tim would share his heart with you, I trust that you too will become a servant of the Lord.

Angus Buchan

PART ONE:
INTRODUCTION

INTRODUCING...

Introductions are important. How we introduce someone not only informs the first impression that others will have of that person, but also reveals how highly (or otherwise) we esteem them. In Africa, we get used to listening to long introductions – the more important the person, the longer the introduction. For high-ranking dignitaries such as royalty or politicians, these are often accompanied by praise-singers who extol the virtues, character and credentials of the individual. Observing protocol carefully is important, particularly when introducing someone who is addressing a formal gathering, a large event, or a conference.

I've had some interesting experiences of being introduced as a speaker. A number of years ago, I was sharing devotions at Message HQ in Manchester, and Andy Hawthorne introduced me by saying, 'This is Tim Tucker, the only person who has consistently refused any job that I've offered them!'

The reality is that I had left the UK in 1998 and was living and ministering in South Africa while Andy was trying to recruit me to come back to the UK to work in Manchester. At the time, I didn't feel that was my calling but, needless to say, Andy thought I was being like Jonah – and told me so! But some years later in 2013, when Andy was in Cape Town exploring his sense that the Lord was leading The Message to open up its first international hub in South Africa, it was clear that God was at last bringing our paths together and I was finally able to accept a job offer from Andy to lead the work in this wonderful country. Now Andy introduces me with far more enthusiasm, and indeed he has been our greatest cheerleader during the initial years of seeing the work established and grow in Cape Town. This book is, in many ways, the result of my journey over the past two decades of seeking to serve God in South Africa. Specifically, it has emerged out of the pioneering stage of establishing Message South Africa as my team and I have sought to answer the question, 'What kind of leaders does God want us to be?'

Another important introduction in my life was from another friend, Jon Burns. Back in 2010, I was involved in spearheading an outreach across South Africa tying in with the FIFA Football World Cup. We facilitated many international groups to come and be involved in what was called 'The Ultimate Goal.' Jon is founder of an organisation called Lionsraw – a network of football fans (originally English football fans) committed to doing good works alongside supporting their team at major football events.[1] In the case of English football fans, who have a bad reputation for drunkenness and violence, this goes against the flow of what is normally expected when they travel to international football events! In 2010, Lionsraw arranged for a team of about 200 English football fans

He doesn't look like

to come to KwaZulu-Natal where they were involved in a number of rural-based projects. I drove down from Pretoria to Durban in order to help with the group's orientation as they prepared to serve. As I stood up to speak at the hotel where they were staying, Jon's introduction of me was short and to the point: 'This is Tim. He doesn't look like much, but he's worth listening to!'

THROUGH THIS BOOK I AM SEEKING TO RE-INTRODUCE YOU TO JESUS

I love the Britishness of this introduction... Jon revealing his honest assessment of me, which the audience (rough and ready British football fans) were probably more likely to heed than if he had given an exaggerated, glowing endorsement. I've come to see, as I've reflected on Jon's words over time, that it is also perhaps the most fitting introduction possible for the central character of this book, Jesus Christ. Through this book I am seeking to re-introduce you to Jesus. This introduction provides a natural critique of much that is written and presented about leadership. The Bible doesn't introduce him as 'Jesus Christ Superstar.' Rather, the consistent testimony of scripture introduces the second person of the Trinity as someone who 'doesn't look like much, but is worth listening to.'

Consider Isaiah 53. The prophet has a vision of the 'suffering servant' who would be the Messiah. Isaiah depicts the servant of God as one who 'had no beauty or majesty to attract us to him, nothing in his appearance that we should desire him' (Is. 53:2). He didn't look like much – the Messiah was not going to be a Hollywood heart-throb or charismatic motivational guru. No, he would serve humanity by carrying our infirmities, sorrows, transgressions, iniquities and punishment. Yet these acts of self-sacrificial service would lead him to ultimate greatness: 'I will give him a portion among the great... for he bore the sin of many and made intercession for the transgressors' (Is. 53:12).

Following Jesus' life, death and resurrection, a hymn of the early church affirms the counter-cultural and revolutionary pathway to greatness that Jesus took. In his letter to the church in Philippi, Paul demonstrates how Jesus chose to be humiliated as the appointed God-man who willingly gave up his rights to equality with God, and 'made himself nothing, taking the very nature of a servant... he humbled himself and became obedient to death – even death on a cross' (Phil. 2:7,9). Again we observe that the pathway of servanthood ultimately led to his exaltation, as God 'gave him the name which is above every name, that at the name of Jesus every knee should bow...' (Phil. 2:9-10).

Which brings us to the title of this book, *Grab A Towel*. During Jesus' life and ministry, his own self-identification was as a servant. He stated it categorically: 'For the Son of Man did not come to be served, but to serve, and to give his life as a ransom for many' (Mark 10:45), and consistently demonstrated it through his actions. Most notably, Jesus' servant-hearted attitude and approach was revealed after a meal with his friends just a couple of days before his crucifixion (see John 13). Jesus poured some water into a basin, grabbed a towel, and started washing the feet of his disciples. This would be a counter-cultural act for any leader to do in any context, but, as we see in Peter's reaction ('No, you shall never wash my feet'), it was shocking in this situation. Yet the Son of God knelt at the feet of those who would soon deny him, flee from him and betray him

JESUS WAS THE ULTIMATE SERVANT LEADER, THE EPITOME OF SERVANTHOOD, AND WE SHOULD ASPIRE TO EMULATE HIS EXAMPLE

to be killed, and washed the Jerusalem muck and dung off their feet. He then rose and said to his disciples these incredible words:

'Do you understand what I have done for you?... You call me "Teacher" and "Lord", and rightly so, for that is what I am. Now that I, your Lord and Teacher, have washed your feet, you also should wash one another's feet. I have set you an example that you should do as I have done for you. Very truly I tell you, no servant is greater than his master, nor is a messenger greater than the one who sent him. Now that you know these things, you will be blessed if you do them.' (John 13:12-17)

Jesus gave his disciples, and all his followers throughout history, a mandate to follow. His example of servant leadership became the benchmark for all Christian leaders, for all time. Jesus was the ultimate servant leader, the epitome of servanthood, and we should aspire to emulate his example.

That's why this book unashamedly introduces Jesus as the central character and model for leadership. To adapt Jon Burns' words, 'This is Jesus Christ. He may not look like much, but follow his example'. After all, this carpenter from a backwater town in Palestine inspired a movement that continues to have ripple effects around the world.

So, grab a towel as we set off to discover what it means to be a Christ-centred servant leader in the 21st century.

GROUND ZERO

INTRODUCING CHRIST-CENTRED SERVANT LEADERSHIP

'We need a new generation of leaders. And we need it now.' – Umair Haque[2]

'For the Son of Man did not come to be served but to serve, and to give his life as a ransom for many.' – Mark 10:45

In 2013, I had the kind of opportunity that doesn't happen often in life – the opportunity of a blank page. At the time I didn't quite see it that way, though. In fact, truth be told, I was still grieving for a vision that I thought had died.

I'd been serving in a Christian non-profit organisation for 12 years. It had been an exciting but challenging period – 12 years of leadership development right at the coal-face. Without dissecting those years (a book in its own right), I felt I was always playing catch-up. I was young when I stepped into leadership. And I was ambitious. As the founder of the first branch of the ministry in

9

South Africa, I remember the excitement I felt when I first saw my name on an org chart as 'Africa Director'– a big title, as Africa is a big place! But I loved the continent and threw myself into the task of overseeing ministry of various forms in 15 different African countries, as well as spearheading the work in South Africa. As a team, we were completely strapped for cash, naïve to the point of folly, but full of passion and zeal for the gospel.

Almost immediately, I began to realise the importance of leadership development. We were attracting young people from different countries who aspired to be leaders. I saw their potential, but was often frustrated at how little I could offer them in terms of time, resources and direct leadership input. But God clearly used this experience to develop my zeal to grow leaders. More and more I began to feel that God was calling me to serve young African leaders, to invest in them so that they could flourish in faith and life.

From 2010 to 2012, I worked with my African leadership team on a strategy that I felt would enable us to develop young leaders across the continent. But the strategy was a big departure from the vision of the organisation as a whole, and it became clear that a transition would soon be required. Although it was a very painful process for many of us involved, in hindsight I see it as part of God's plan to draw me into something new.

By early 2013, it was clear that my time with the organisation had come to an end. I felt a bit like Elijah when he fled from Ahab and Jezebel – needing to get away from it all and hear from God again, and simply needing some rest. I resigned without a clue as to where God would lead me next. Although I had strong feelings of grief, loss and failure, I also felt a sense of relief and anticipation.

I was at ground zero. I had a blank page. An opportunity to start over.

Daunting as it seemed, it also felt good to have the space to consider how I could proactively develop a ministry that would move forward in strength. I also took this time to complete my first book, *The Pace Setter*, which helped cement my approach to leadership development as I explored the relationship between Paul and Timothy. I began my PhD which explored the topic of leadership within the context of sports ministry in South Africa. It was exciting fuel for me as I began to get clarity on my next assignment.

And in the middle of this process, I finally felt ready to respond positively to Andy Hawthorne's invitation to join The Message and spearhead their first international hub in Cape Town. God also graciously provided continuity as two former colleagues joined me for this next adventure.

BECOMING CHRIST-CENTRED SERVANT LEADERS

Part of the blessing of finding ourselves at ground zero was a chance for our small, pioneering team to define the kind of leaders we wanted to be. This book is a consequence of that process, as it was then we decided to become 'Christ-centred servant leaders.' The eight hallmarks of Christ-centred servant leadership presented in the pages that follow are those that have come alive to us as we have embarked on the adventure of leadership within the context of The Message in South Africa, as we seek to raise a movement of leaders from the margins of society amongst the outcasts, prisoners and gang members. Clearly, they are drawn from my past experiences of ministry in Africa. Yet they are also fashioned from the process of becoming part of The Message global family and imbibing the DNA of this extraordinary organisation.

It's important to say these hallmarks have emerged as part of a collaborative process. Firstly, with my co-director here in Cape Town, Mark Slessenger, who helped me develop the outline and deliver training to our South African leadership team. Secondly, they've been developed through leadership mentoring groups that I've facilitated over the past few years – sharing these concepts, receiving feedback, and honing my understanding of what it means to be a Christ-centred servant leader. And thirdly, they've been tried and tested through countless interactions and discussions with good friends and co-leaders over many years.

It sometimes appears that much leadership material is written in a vacuum – but no one leads in a vacuum. This book is seeking to apply the hallmarks of Christ-centred servant leadership within the context of leading a contemporary mission organisation. We're seeking to answer the questions, 'How do we follow Jesus' example within the context of leading a 21st-century organisation?' and 'How do we become the kind of leaders that are worth following?'

This book seeks to help you ask the right questions that will enable you to follow Jesus as you lead within your particular context. I invite you to grab a towel and join me back at ground zero, as we look afresh at the example of Christ, in order to discern how his example of servant leadership can shape and correct our approach to leadership.

THE LOST ART OF LEADERSHIP

Umair Haque wrote, 'We need a new generation of leaders. And we need it now ... Leadership – true leadership – is a lost art.'[3]

I agree! We need a new generation of leaders, and we need them to lead based on ancient principles applied within the challenges of our modern world. There's no shortage of books and courses on leadership, but this one seeks to present how The Message Trust, as an international Christian mission organisation, seeks to follow Jesus Christ's model of leadership among hard-to-reach urban youth in cities around the world. We seek to rediscover the 'lost art of leadership', not as an academic theory, but earthed in the practical realities

WE SERVE AS A SIGNPOST TOWARDS THE GREATEST AND MOST INFLUENTIAL LEADER IN HISTORY

that leaders face day by day. We trust this book can be helpful to all leaders, not because we have all the answers, but because we serve as a signpost towards the greatest and most influential leader in history – the one who spoke the words every Christian leader should emulate: 'That is what the Son of Man has done: He came to serve, not be served – and then to give away his life in exchange for the many who are held hostage' (Matt. 20:28, MSG).

John Maxwell once famously said, 'Everything rises and falls on leadership',[4] reflecting the almost cult-like status assigned to leaders and leadership in recent years. One can understand and even adopt the sentiment of this statement, but it needs to be clarified: everything rises on *the right kind* of leadership. This book will attempt to explore what that looks like, and present conclusions that are counter-cultural amidst much of prevailing leadership theory. These hallmarks are presented as signposts for you to explore further what it means to become a Christ-centred leader, within your context, and to discern how to become a servant leader on behalf of those you influence on a daily basis.

This book presents an approach to leadership development that has been birthed out of the experience of The Message Trust as an innovative and rapidly-expanding Christian mission organisation. We have seen that effective leadership is essential if we are to fulfil our vision to reach tens of thousands of young people from tough urban neighbourhoods around the world. We also believe that, in Jesus, we have the model leader to emulate and shape our approach to leadership.

Here's what Andy Hawthorne, our Founder and CEO, has to say about leadership:

> A true leader is not someone with a business card that says 'Chief Executive', 'Senior Pastor' or the like, but an individual who, when they look over their shoulder, has lots of people following them. For Christians, of course, a true leader is someone who can say, like Paul, 'Don't just follow me, but follow me as I follow Christ.'

Many great leaders are true one-offs and we're naïve to think that if we simply do what they have done, we'll achieve what they have achieved. But with Jesus Christ, it's a different story. That's because we don't just get the world's greatest leadership manual in the pages of scripture, but the opportunity to actually live out and multiply ministry the way he did by the power of the Spirit within us. When Jesus breathed on the disciples and said 'As the Father sent me, I am sending you' he really meant it, not just for them, but for us in the 21st century, too.

People have been kind enough to say that over the last few decades, The Message has been instrumental in setting the pace for mission in words and actions. Whether that's true or not, you can't argue with the fact that we all need to step up the pace of multiplying leaders if we are going to fulfil the mission God has given us.[5]

Leading within the context of an organisation like The Message provides a useful critique, or alternative, to much of the leadership material that is currently available. Much of it seems to focus on investing in high achievers who, so it is believed, have the capacity to operate in the upper echelons of business, politics and the church, in order to bring about tangible change through a 'drip-down' approach. But we believe that leadership is not about hierarchy or job titles, or that it's purely for those with charisma or exceptional giftedness. Our understanding is that anyone who is part of The Message is serving in some leadership capacity, by exerting an influence towards our overarching goal of raising up generations of urban heroes. Our intention is to empower all our staff and volunteers to become the best leaders they can be in order to have the maximum impact for the kingdom as Christ-centred servant leaders.

We see this particularly strongly in South Africa, where our staff is made up of almost 50% former gang members or prisoners. Clearly, our leadership development pipeline is not typical of most organisations! However, it is perhaps more in line with Jesus' approach to invest in 'unschooled and ordinary men' who went on to change the world (see, for instance, Acts 4:13).[6] For me, grabbing a towel means that I daily seek to wash the feet of people who have done some terrible things in their past, but in whom I see incredible potential to become transformational leaders, and impact society in ways others never could.

THREE KEYS FOR LEADERSHIP DEVELOPMENT

As I have worked with emerging leaders, I have discerned three principles foundational to the approach to positive leadership development. These will form the basis of the *Grab A Towel* interaction materials on our dedicated website, *www.grabatowel.site*.

THE LEADERS' TABLE: GROWTH THROUGH MUTUAL LEARNING AND SUPPORT

The first principle is based on a concept I call 'The Leaders' Table.' Leaders don't emerge or grow simply by having a leadership 'expert' provide teaching and instruction to a group of students. Rather, growth in leadership comes through 'doing life together'– literally, sitting round a table (preferably over a meal) and engaging deeply, holding one another accountable, and encouraging one another to become more proficient leaders. The table is a place of mutual submission and respect, where each person can grow to become a better leader within their sphere of influence. The Leaders' Table takes development seriously – recognising there is no simple formula for success, but instead requiring a commitment from each person to seek to learn from others and willingly share their experiences to enable and empower them to grow.

The inspiration for the concept of The Leaders' Table derives from a leadership hero of mine in the Old Testament: Nehemiah. The first five chapters of the book of Nehemiah show how God moved in his heart to accept a massive leadership challenge – to rebuild the ruins of Jerusalem. Against all odds and in the face of severe opposition, Nehemiah mobilises the Jews to accomplish a superhuman feat – rebuilding the walls in just 52 days. There are undoubtedly many ingredients to Nehemiah's success, but one key factor is highlighted in Nehemiah 5:14-19. Nehemiah, as governor of Judah, makes a conscious decision not to lead as previous governors who use their leadership position for personal gain by placing heavy financial burdens on the people. Rather, he uses his position to serve and empower the officials and leaders by gathering them together and providing a meal for them every day. This daily *braai* (South African for 'barbecue') brings together not only the Judean leaders, but also leaders from surrounding nations.

Here Nehemiah's leadership philosophy is laid bare. Unlike his predecessors in Jerusalem, or contemporary leaders in other nations of his day, he isn't interested in what he could receive. He doesn't abuse his position of power, or 'lord over people,' to line his pockets. There is no nepotism or narcissism. Instead, he goes completely against the culture of leadership in his day and lays a table from which other leaders can eat, fellowship, collaborate, learn, and be encouraged. Furthermore, he provides for this daily event from his own pocket. In other words, he provides a platform – literally, lays a table of provision – for other leaders to succeed. Nehemiah's leaders' table was a daily event for 150 Jews, officials and those from other nations. I like to imagine what it must have been like to be at that daily meal as leaders gathered, shared, celebrated, wept and encouraged one another in the daily challenges that they faced.

Leaders in the 21st century face the same challenges that Nehemiah did 2,500 years ago. There is clearly a lack of godly leadership in the world as many seek to attain positions of influence for personal gain. I believe that there is an emerging generation of leaders who will not settle for the status quo. But they cannot stand in isolation. I want to encourage you as you read this book to gather around a table with other leaders and begin to share together on the tragedies and triumphs that you are facing in leadership. Follow Nehemiah's example and take the initiative! Use the discussion questions in the *Interaction* section on our website, *grabatowel.site*, for more ideas.

This book has emerged as a result of Leaders' Table groups that I have personally led over the past four years (always around a meal). We have discussed the concepts presented in this book and the contribution of my fellow leaders has indelibly shaped my approach to leadership – and the book you are now reading.

BECOMING DEEP WELLS OF RESOURCE

The second principle I have discovered is that of 'The Deep Well.' The challenge in the world today is that many leaders resemble shallow wells – they offer short-term solutions but their impact soon runs dry, with their sphere of influence regressing to a state of spiritual drought. The Deep Wells principle is all about long-term, community-based, sustained ministry – going deep before going broad.

When I was at ground zero, God spoke to me very specifically about this principle. I was reading about Isaac's experience in Genesis 26:19-22. Isaac, Abraham's son, had been living in the land of the Philistines during a time of famine. Having prospered, King Abimelech asks him to move on from there – so Isaac travels into the Valley of Gerar and starts re-opening wells that his father had dug in that area. As he goes from place to place, Isaac experiences opposition from local herders. Each time he moves on, until he finally comes to a place where he opens up

DEEP WELL LEADERS ENABLE OTHERS TO FLOURISH – THEY PROVIDE A SUSTAINED SOURCE OF SPIRITUAL WATER

a well and no one opposes him. The Bible says that he named it Rehoboth, saying, 'Now the Lord has given us room and we will flourish in the land.'

God spoke to me from this text as we embarked upon launching The Message in South Africa. Just as Isaac reopened a well that became a spacious place of resource and enabled him to flourish in the land, so we believe God has called The Message to be a deep well of resource to enable our team, our leaders, to flourish in the land. Our task is to provide leaders with the space to thrive and the opportunities to grow in order that they themselves can become deep wells of resource and effectively serve Christ in this generation.

Deep Well leaders enable others to flourish – they provide a sustained source of spiritual water that can enable fruitful and productive living for generations of people. I believe this is the kind of leader that God wants all of us to become.

My prayer is that this book might become a deep well of resource that will enable you to grow, too. As you go deeper, so you will become a spring of life that can resource others. Deep Well leaders continue to grow as lifelong learners which is why, in the *Interaction* section on our website, *grabatowel.site*, I've also highlighted additional resources for further reading.

EVERYONE IS A LEADER, EVERYONE IS A FOLLOWER

The third principle is that followership is as important as leadership. To be a great leader, you firstly need to be a great follower. This principle permeates all the material in this book and could be summed up by the Apostle Paul's words, 'Follow my example as I follow the example of Christ' (1 Cor. 11:1). Paul became arguably the greatest Christian leader in history because he was firstly the greatest *follower* in Christian history. Paul took Christ's own words seriously: 'If anyone would come after me, let him deny himself and take up his cross and follow me' (Luke 9:23 ESV).

Our effectiveness in leadership will be directly proportional to our commitment to followership. This begins by counting the cost of submitting daily to Christ, which is the very essence of servant leadership. We can only lead others because we are serving Christ, and in serving Christ we learn that the only true form of leadership is servanthood. As Jesus said, 'Whoever wants to be great among you must be your servant, and whoever wants to be first must be slave of all. For even the Son of Man did not come to be served, but to serve, and to give his life as a ransom for many' (Mark 10:44-45).

An important part of serving others is recognising that we also need to follow others. Later in the book we will discuss the concept of 'rotational functional leadership.' This is essentially the willingness to forgo a position of leadership in order to follow someone who is better suited to leading in a particular situation. Again, followership is not about hierarchy, rank, or titles – it is a matter of the heart and a matter of humility. It is also an acknowledgement that God gifts individuals with unique experiences that he intends to use in his kingdom when those experiences can provide leadership and benefit to others.

This is counter-cultural, and it is often costly. But as we saw in the example of Nehemiah, we need to become leaders who are willing to make the necessary sacrifices in order to get the job done. We need leaders who are not motivated by material gain or earthly power but have a deep, intrinsic desire to serve others. I trust that this book will inspire you to grow as a Christ-centred servant leader as you yourself draw closer to Christ.

Because followership is so critical for great leadership, the *Interaction* section on our website, *grabatowel.site*, will provide you with some practical ways that you can apply the hallmarks of servant leadership to becoming a better follower.

THE *GRAB A TOWEL* LEADERSHIP COMMITMENT

This book flows from the experiences I have gained at The Message, seeking to develop a leadership philosophy which we trust will be integral to the DNA of our organisation. This will be expressed in the *Grab A Towel* commitment at the end of this book. It is my hope that each person who reads this book will develop their own leadership philosophy that applies and adapts what is presented in these pages to their own lives, calling and context. We trust that this process will catalyse imaginative and prayerful engagement that opens up new horizons for leaders in the 21st century.

Becoming a Christ-centred servant leader is a lifelong process that needs to be constantly nurtured – it's a destination we continually move towards as we become more like Jesus. I hope that the material in this book aids you in your journey and that the leadership charter after the last chapter provides aspirations that will encourage you to keep growing as a Christ-centred servant leader.

Practically, this book focuses on eight hallmarks of servant leadership which we seek to grow in throughout our lives. The individual chapters in this book correspond to each of these areas.

1. Focus on character (Chapter 1)
2. Develop a prophetic vision (Chapter 2)
3. Maintain faithful stewardship (Chapter 3)
4. Become deep wells (Chapter 4)
5. Put people first (Chapter 5)
6. Give power away (Chapter 6)
7. Lead with compassion (Chapter 7)
8. Have steel in your spine (Chapter 8)

SERVANT LEADERSHIP PERSONIFIED

'What counts in life is not the mere fact that we have lived. It is what difference we have made to the lives of others that will determine the significance of the life we lead' – Nelson Mandela[7]

'We have different gifts, according to the grace given to each of us. If your gift is prophesying, then prophesy in accordance with your faith; if it is serving, then serve; if it is teaching, then teach; if it is to encourage, then give encouragement; if it is giving, then give generously; if it is to lead, do it diligently; if it is to show mercy, do it cheerfully.' – Romans 12:6-8

True servant leadership is most powerful when it's experienced, rather than merely expressed in words. South African President Nelson Mandela is revered as a global example of leadership in the face of adversity. Countless books have been written on the lessons to be learned from his reconciliatory humility and strength of character. For me, two snapshots from his life demonstrate these qualities in particular, as he recognised the responsibility that came with his position of influence, and how he shaped the response of a generation of subjugated South Africans.

At the height of the apartheid regime, Mandela was one of several accused in the Rivonia Trial between October 9, 1963 and June 12, 1964. There was a very real possibility that the chief activists in the anti-apartheid movement would be executed as the National Party sought to silence all opposition to their white-elitist regime. On April 20, 1964 it was the turn of Nelson Mandela to testify. A qualified lawyer, his meticulously prepared speech explained his actions, exposed the injustices of apartheid, and rationally argued for regime change in South Africa by any means possible. Mandela was acutely aware that most of what he said would confirm the assessment of those in power of him as a dangerous terrorist. Yet Mandela saw beyond that. He wasn't just speaking to the courtroom – he was speaking to his people. More than that, he was speaking to the whole nation. In closing his speech, he gave an insight into his character and vision for South Africa... he was not a terrorist bent on violent revolution, but a human being dedicated to restoring dignity to all the people of South Africa. He said:

> During my lifetime I have dedicated myself to this struggle of the African people. I have fought against

white domination, and I have fought against black domination. I have cherished the ideal of a democratic and free society in which all persons live together in harmony and with equal opportunities. It is an ideal which I hope to live for and to achieve. But if needs be, it is an ideal for which I am prepared to die.[8]

Mandela's leadership mastery is seen in this short extract. He was first of all leading *himself* – prepared to make the ultimate sacrifice in order to see his dream fulfilled. He was also leading *his movement* – the ANC – who had formed the Freedom Charter and were committed to fulfilling the ideals embodied in that document. Furthermore, he was providing leadership to *the subjugated people of South Africa*, those who may not have been ANC members, but with whom he could identify because of the injustice of their situation. But, critically, he was also leading *his oppressors*. He rose above their hate and prejudice in order to paint a picture of a new South Africa that would free the oppressor from their hatred, and usher in a new era of freedom for all.

We need to jump forward 30 years to 1994 for the second example of his influence in action. Mandela had spent 27 years in prison, and undergone incredible suffering, yet did not compromise on his dream. Formerly an accused man in a trial that could have resulted in his execution, he was now the president of his country and in leadership over those who had oppressed him, tortured his family and killed his friends. Once again, Mandela shone as a beacon of servant leadership – able to put aside any desire for vindication and revenge, and instead focus on the hope that his dream of a free and democratic country was now becoming a reality. In his inaugural speech as president he said the following:

We enter into a covenant that we shall build a society in which all South Africans, both black and white, will be able to walk tall, without any fear in their hearts, assured of their inalienable right to human dignity – a rainbow nation at peace with itself and the world...

Today we are entering a new era for our country and its people. Today we celebrate not the victory of a party, but a victory for all the people of South Africa.[9]

Mandela's victory was a victory of servant leadership and his example has become synonymous with the definition of a servant leader.

It is abundantly clear from Mandela's example that leadership always focuses on others. As a mission movement, The Message is focused on others, too. The main purpose of our organisation is to present the gospel to the least, the last and the lost, and to see them become transformational leaders. We are leading in that direction and everything we do will be evaluated against the goal of raising up generations of urban heroes. Our leadership is not defined by how well we run the organisation, whether we are financially viable, or even if we have the funkiest programmes in the city. We are ultimately a movement of people with a gospel goal – the belief that God wants all people to be saved.

WHAT'S SO SPECIAL ABOUT BIBLICAL LEADERSHIP?

This is an important question. There are clearly many great leaders who are not Christians and it is true to say that Christians can learn from leadership lessons drawn from secular sources and examples (and in this book I draw from a variety of sources). However, if our goal is to have a spiritual impact in the world, we need to consider how to differentiate our leadership, given that the Christian mission is ultimately committed to gospel-centred outcomes.

Romans 12:8 lists leadership as a gift given for the service of God's church, and notes that if someone's gift is leadership, then they should govern diligently. There is clearly a gift and calling available to Christian leaders – a calling to be servant leaders who are empowered by the Holy Spirit in order to lead effectively. Henry and Richard Blackaby helpfully define spiritual leadership as simply 'moving people on to God's agenda.'[10] And that's what Christ-centred servant leadership does. Leadership always comes with an assignment – it is not purely a position for a position's sake. Our assignment as Christian leaders is to move people from the point where they are at, towards an encounter with Jesus Christ which equips them to live wholeheartedly for him in the world in the service of others.

This is the crux of Christ-centred servant-leadership, and this book aims to equip you for your specific task as a servant leader.

DO WE LEAD FIRST OR SERVE FIRST?

The primary focus of a servant leader is that they are committed to serving others first, not leading others. Their primary intent is to serve, and their focus is on being a servant and a steward, not a leader or an owner.[11] Servant leadership became a common phrase

following the writings of Robert Greenleaf in the 1970s. He wrote
the following:

> The servant-leader is servant first... It begins with the
> natural feeling that one wants to serve, to serve first.
> Then conscious choice brings one to aspire to lead.
> That person is sharply different from one who is leader
> first, perhaps because of the need to assuage an unusual
> power drive or to acquire material possessions... The
> leader-first and the servant-first are two extreme types.
> Between them there are shadings and blends that are
> part of the infinite variety of human nature.[12]

This table shows the contrast between a leader focused on leading
first, versus a leader focused on serving first:

LEADS FIRST	SERVES FIRST
Vision is for self-advancement	Vision is for the common good
Leads from power through position	Leads through people from relationship
Followers are a means to an end	Followers are valued of highest importance
Focus is self	Focus is others
Promotes own agenda	Listens and welcomes feedback

Surrounded by 'yes-men'	Values different opinions
Prioritises projects	Invests in people
Autocratic	Accountable
Influences from fear	Influences from trust
Selfish ambition	Self-sacrificial
Success = fulfilling own agenda	Success = others fulfil potential

The contrast between those who lead first against those who serve first can be most helpfully defined in terms of aspirations. Although Christians can aspire to be leaders, their motivation must be driven by their heart to serve, not merely leading for leading's sake. A Christian leader aspires to serve Christ by serving others. Their position of leadership provides opportunity for service.

THE PRIMARY FOCUS OF A SERVANT LEADER IS THAT THEY ARE COMMITTED TO SERVING OTHERS FIRST, NOT LEADING OTHERS

I believe that Greenleaf's understanding of servant leadership needs to be rediscovered in the 21st century and applied through the lens of Jesus Christ. As we have already seen, Jesus was the ultimate servant leader, the world's greatest leader and the epitome of servanthood.

In the film *The Passion of the Christ*,[13] there is a powerful scene depicting servant leadership. It depicts Jesus being whipped and beaten by a Roman soldier. He is lying on the ground, bloodied and in agony. Semi-conscious, he rolls on his side and sees the sandals of his persecutor... and the scene shifts as Jesus' mind recalls his final gathering with the disciples as he knelt and washed their sandaled feet. In that moment we are reminded that Christ's act of servanthood, when he grabbed a towel and knelt at his disciples' feet, was a metaphor for his ultimate act of service. As our loving friend, he willingly took the punishment that we all deserved for the wrong things we have done. Jesus, although innocent of any wrongdoing, paid the ultimate price. Just as he demonstrated his love by washing his disciples' feet, we also recognise that he loved the Roman soldier who beat him, Pilate who handed him over for crucifixion, and all of us who were represented by the crowds who either jeered or stood idly by as the Son of God succumbed to death.

Our motivation as servant leaders in following Jesus' example is, therefore, not simply that he grabbed a towel and washed the disciples' feet, but in that through his act of self-sacrifice on the cross he effectively washes our feet *every day* of the muck and dung of our wrong actions, thoughts and motives. And, even though we may not feel qualified, he commissions us to follow his example and serve others as he has served us. When it cost him so much, how can we refuse?

Jesus is passing the towel to us. Let's learn how to follow his example.

PART TWO:
EIGHT HALLMARKS OF SERVANT LEADERS

CHAPTER 1

FOCUS ON CHARACTER

CHRIST-CENTRED SERVANT LEADERS INCREASINGLY DISPLAY THE CHARACTER OF CHRIST

'Mature ministry flows from a mature character, formed in the graduate school of life.' – Robert Clinton[14]

'He made himself nothing by taking the very nature of a servant, being made in human likeness...' – Philippians 2:7

The Superhero movie is a film genre that still reliably draws crowds to the cinema. The depiction of a person with superhuman powers, willing to battle for justice against forces of evil, has been a winning formula on screen for over a century. But in recent times I've noticed that there has been a significant shift in the way super-heroes are portrayed.

Throughout the 20th century, superheroes in comic books and on the big screen not only protected the innocent and fought injustice, they were also moral guardians, demonstrating virtue and ethical excellence. I recently re-watched the classic Superman films from the 1970s and 80s with my children, and I was struck by how Superman not only had super-human powers but also a superior moral code to the mere mortals of Planet Earth.

This is no longer the case. Today superheroes are not the squeaky-clean role models of yesteryear, nor are they every mother's dream date for their daughter. They are given significant character flaws, portrayed as far-from-perfect human beings who just happen (or indeed, happen to have been cursed) to possess special powers or talents that enable them to save the world. More alarmingly, modern superheroes seem to possess no qualms about the measures required to accomplish their goal of defeating their nemesis. They seem oblivious to the collateral damage that accompanies their objective whereby the ends (defeating the bad guy) justifies the means (extreme violence and destruction). The message which seems to be communicated today is that good character and moral fibre are now equated with weakness. Superheroes are tough individuals who have been through the school of hard knocks and often emerge as reluctant heroes who are dealing with their own demons and issues through their schizophrenic existence.

Unfortunately, this attraction to superhero-type leaders with flawed characters extends beyond the fantasy world of Marvel or DC comics – it is also reflected in modern-day leaders of major corporates, sports teams and political parties. Character is regularly sacrificed on the altar of pragmatism as contemporary culture overlooks moral conduct or ethical considerations if opinion-formers believe there is a greater good at stake.

In contrast, I believe that character remains the number one priority for leaders:

Character before Charisma: charisma can be instrumental in building a following. But charisma without character means people can get hurt by a leader who uses them to fulfil his or her own dreams and vision.

Character before Competence: competence is critical and leaders should seek to grow across multiple areas of competency. However, competence without character can lead to pride – the most destructive influence upon a leader.

Character before Credentials: titles, qualifications, and a proven track record can all be important in establishing credibility – but they remain secondary to having a Christ-like character which causes a leader to depend completely on God and not on his credentials.

Charisma, competence and credentials... all can build a leader's reputation, but it is having the character of Christ formed within us that will ensure that these are held in perspective, and enable a leader to engage in building the kingdom of God, not their own empire.

THE CHARACTER OF CHRIST

There is a stark contrast between the modern-day Hollywood superhero, business tycoon or political powerhouse and the central figure of this book – Jesus Christ. In order to become a Christ-centred servant leader we need to understand the character of Christ. Jesus wasn't a superhero – he was a servant. In his letter to the church in Philippi, Paul shares what most commentators believe to be a hymn of the early church. It poignantly reveals the character of Christ and demonstrates the contrast between Jesus and the superhero-type leader:

> Your attitude should be the same as that of Christ Jesus: who, being in very nature God, did not consider equality with God something to be used to his own advantage; rather, he made himself nothing by taking the very nature of a servant, being made in human likeness. And being found in appearance as a man, he humbled himself by becoming obedient to death – even death on a cross! (Phil. 2:6-9)

Paul is presenting Jesus as the example that all Christians should follow. In the preceding verses he exhorts believers towards love, support and mutual submission. Then he states that, in order to achieve this level of unity, it is critical that believers foster the same attitude as Jesus Christ. It was Jesus' attitude that enabled him to fulfil his calling. Jesus, the Son of God, obediently submitted himself to the will of God and gave up his equality in the Godhead in order to become a servant. The passage says he had the 'nature of a servant'. In other words, his character – to the very core – was that of a servant. His character was defined by his willingness to submit to God's purpose for his life through serving others.

Out of his obedience to the Father and out of love for humanity, Jesus chose to humble himself and die the cruellest of deaths as the victim of Roman capital punishment. The verses then go on to reveal the result of his obedience: God exalted him to the highest place and all people will one day acknowledge his lordship and glory.

Christ could not have fulfilled his destiny if his character had contradicted his calling. Likewise, for Christian leaders in the 21st century, our attitude has to be the same as Jesus Christ if we desire to fulfil our calling. It all begins with having the same nature as Christ – having his DNA written into ours. Therefore, forming a Christ-like character must be an absolute priority if we are to become Christ-centred servant leaders.

STRENGTH TO SERVE

Critically, we need to recognise that being a servant cannot be equated with weakness. Sen Sendjaya and James Sarros write:

> Contrary to the popular opinion of the day, Jesus taught that a leader's greatness is measured by a total commitment to serve fellow human beings... it was not weakness that compelled Jesus to be a servant... Servant leaders portray a resolute conviction and strong character by taking on not only the role of a servant but also the nature of a servant.[15]

Great leaders need to have strength and resolve. However, the strength and resolve that servant leaders demonstrate is to be committed to go against the flow and serve people, even at great personal cost. As I seek to identify emerging leaders within The Message, I have learned not to look for super-human leaders who exhibit extraordinary abilities that enable them to single-handedly solve every problem. Equally, servant leadership doesn't mean that leaders are walkovers – wet blankets who do not proactively respond to the challenges of leadership. Jesus demonstrated his strength by becoming a servant. This is what it means to be a Christ-centred servant-leader – to be willing to count the cost and do what it takes in order to serve others. Indeed, it takes strength of character to be a Christ-like servant leader. Therefore, Christ-centred servant leaders need to prioritise getting to know Jesus better in order that his character is formed within them so that they can selflessly serve others.

NINE MARKS OF THE CHARACTER OF A SERVANT LEADER

The following acrostic for the word 'character' outlines the nine distinguishing marks of the character of servant leaders I have recognised as priority areas for character development for those of us seeking to be servant leaders. Christ-like servant leaders are:

Content
Humble
Accountable
Reliable
Approachable
Consistent
Trustworthy
Exemplary
Respectful

This is by no means an exhaustive list, but provides an initial biblical framework for Christ-like character development. Let's look at them one by one.

CONTENT

This mark of a servant leader is of primary importance because it stands in stark contrast to the materialistic culture of our generation. We live in a world where people are constantly seeking the next thing: whether materially, experientially, or relationally. The sad reality is that many people are discontented with their lot in life, always pursuing an elusive happiness they hope to find elsewhere. It was no different in New Testament times: in the Parable of the Sower in Matthew 13, Jesus taught that the deceitfulness of wealth and the desire for 'things' can choke people on their spiritual journey.

> **IT TAKES STRENGTH OF CHARACTER TO BE A CHRIST-LIKE SERVANT LEADER**

Paul demonstrated the counter-cultural nature of the gospel when he stated, 'I have learned the secret of being content in any and every situation, whether well fed or hungry, whether living in plenty or in want' (Phil. 4:12). Paul remarks that contentment is a 'secret'... indicating it is an elusive quality that few experience in this world. It is in the context of being content in all situations that Paul then states he can do all things through Christ who gives him strength (Phil. 4:13). Often this verse is used as a motivational mantra to help Christians get through tough times or face difficult situations. While God surely does enable Christians to persevere through trying times, Paul clearly has in mind that the goal is not to find a way to merely survive or get through the different challenges in life, but to actually find contentment in whatever life throws at us. Leaders can have the confidence to face whatever challenges may face them if they have learned the secret of contentment.

The fruit of contentment is peace. Jesus taught, 'Blessed are the peacemakers for they will be called children of God' (Matt. 5:9). As the character of Christ is formed within them, Christ-centred servant leaders will increasingly become men and women of peace, demonstrating that they are indeed children of God.

HUMBLE

In the verse preceding the hymn exalting Christ's character discussed earlier, Paul writes, 'Do nothing out of selfish ambition or vain conceit. Rather, in humility value others above your-selves' (Phil. 2:3). Pride is a destructive force that corrodes the effectiveness of leaders. Christ-like leaders will be humble leaders – anything else is a contradiction. As I have observed humble leaders, I've noticed that they usually exhibit three related characteristics.

Firstly, humble leaders have a right view of themselves. In the verse Paul says that we must do nothing out of selfish ambition nor be motivated by vanity. This is an important consideration today in a world of social media and self-branding, where the emphasis is on self-promotion and assertion. Human beings are intrinsically self-centred and self-obsessed and Christian leaders will inevitably face the temptation of pride. Servant leaders should foster a correct view of themselves... recognising their limitations, sinfulness and complete dependence on the grace of God. If Jesus Christ, the Son of God, chose humility over fame, then how much more should his imperfect servants seek to follow his example? This does not mean self-deprecation – which would be a denial of being made in the image of God. Christian leaders must have a right view of self that acknowledges that, when dependent upon God, we are able to serve him faithfully and fulfil his calling upon our lives.

Secondly, humble leaders have a desire to serve others. As well as having a right view of ourselves, it is critical to have a right view of others. Paul states that our view of others must be that we consider them better than ourselves. This is radical, counter-intuitive self-denial, but it is also a simple choice that we must make every day. Servant leadership requires that we think of other people as worthy of our service. To think others worthy of our service involves genuinely loving other people.

Thirdly, humble leaders choose to do humble things. This is where the rubber hits the road. Humility is about actions. If you desire to be a humble person the secret is not to pray more, read more, or think more about it. The secret is to actively do things that are, in some senses, humiliating! This can be practically applied at home, at work or at church – do the things that others don't want to do. Don't just stick to your own job description – take on tasks that you are over-qualified for. Do the menial things, the dirty things, the things that no one will see. Don't seek praise, do it in secret. If you want to be humble, then do humble things.

ACCOUNTABLE

In Proverbs 27:17, King Solomon says: 'As iron sharpens iron, so one person sharpens another.' Character formation requires the input of other people. With all the dangers and temptations associated with leadership in the 21st century, it is critical that those of us in Christian leadership surround ourselves with people who are willing to speak truthfully to us and hold us accountable for our actions and attitudes. Oscar Wilde is attributed as saying, 'true friends stab you in the front'. Becoming Christ-centred servant leaders necessitates that we build relationships with people who hold us to account. This is a key mark of servant leadership and is further explored in Chapter 4.

RELIABLE

The Apostle Paul's protégé was Timothy, someone he invested in over many years. One thing Paul impressed upon Timothy was that he himself had to invest in other leaders. In advising Timothy, he highlighted the kind of character he should look for in emerging leaders. In 2 Timothy 2:2, Paul writes: 'And the things you have heard me say in the presence of many witnesses entrust to reliable people who will also be qualified to teach others.' Reliability is the key character quality that Paul seems to value above others. Let's face it, reliability is not really considered a 'sexy' quality. They don't write books or make movies about reliable people. When people think of reliability they may think of their faithful dog or the 15-year-old German-made car that consistently chugs along and never breaks down. But reliability, and its related qualities of faithfulness, consistency and stability, is exactly the quality that Paul looked for in emerging leaders.

I can understand why Paul so valued this quality. It is incredibly reassuring to be surrounded by reliable people. It can be quite the opposite if we are always unsure of how others will respond. We find ourselves on tenterhooks if we are uncertain when someone is going to explode, lose their temper, or simply not show up. Becoming a Christ-like servant leader involves being a reliable, dependable, and faithful person – someone who will stay the course, remain committed to scripture and persevere through the good times and the bad.

APPROACHABLE

I think Jesus was the most approachable man to have ever lived. Consider what it was like for him when he walked the earth. Crowds followed him. The sick reached out to touch him. His disciples kept asking stupid questions. He was constantly in demand. And the reason he was in demand? He was approachable: people felt they could approach him, engage him, ask him questions and make demands of him.[16] Indeed, Jesus did not place limits upon his approachability. Consider his promise in Matthew 11:28-30: 'Come to me, all you who are weary and burdened, and I will give you rest.'

Christ-centred servant leaders have Jesus' character formed within them in direct proportion to daily approaching Jesus and laying our burdens upon him. As we do that, we have the capacity to become approachable to others. One of the hardest things about being approachable is that it means people will find it easy to share their grievances, pain and disappointment with us. As leaders, we need to be sure that we are able to accept criticism and things spoken in 'tough love' with humbleness and gentleness. Too often it is easy to become defensive and react negatively when people say tough things to us. The problem is that if we react in this way, then people will be reluctant to be truthful with us in the future.

An approachable leader will cultivate an environment of truthfulness. Being approachable is a mark of a leader who is submitted to Christ and secure in their relationship with him and, therefore, able to accept both praise and criticism equally with grace and humility.

CONSISTENT

Christ-like servant leaders will always show consistency between their words and their actions. Inconsistent leaders are quick to boast about what they can do, but they fail to back it up with actions. They over-promise and under-deliver. Christ-like servant leaders will consistently over-deliver because they do not make promises that they cannot keep!

Henry and Richard Blackaby give an insight on the connection between consistency and integrity and why this is so essential for Christian leaders:

> Integrity means being consistent in one's behaviour under every circumstance, including those unguarded moments. If leaders are normally peaceable and well mannered, but they throw violent temper tantrums when things go wrong, their lives lack integrity. If leaders are honest and moral in public, but discard those standards in private, their lives lack integrity. When leaders have integrity, their followers always know what to expect.[17]

That closing statement is critical! When leaders are consistent, it puts their followers at ease because they know what to expect. Inconsistency undermines trust. Consistency builds trust and is critical in building cohesive teams. Which leads neatly to...

TRUSTWORTHY

In Luke 19:11-27, Jesus tells a parable that contrasts two trust-worthy servants with an untrustworthy one. Jesus commends the servants who had been trustworthy in small matters, stating that they would now be entrusted with greater responsibility. Becoming a faithful, trustworthy leader will be a theme that is developed later in this book and specifically considered in Chapter 5.

Nothing destroys leadership quicker than breaking trust. It takes a long time to build trust, and it can be broken in a moment. Being trustworthy is therefore critical to becoming a Christ-centred servant leader. Equally critical is to place trust in others. Cultivating an environment of trust is a two-way street. Leaders require the trust of their followers in order to fulfil a God-given vision; equally, servant leaders will trust their followers as those that God has placed within their care and through whom God will fulfil his plans and purposes.

EXEMPLARY

Becoming a Christ-centred servant leader is all about following the example of Christ. Once again, we remember Jesus' words: 'I have set you an example that you should do as I have done for you' (John 13:15). We are to grab a towel and follow his example. It is humbling, and at times scary, to recognise that people are watching us, examining us, critiquing us, and that we are on earth as Christ's representatives. Therefore, we should aspire to display exemplary conduct as his ambassadors (2 Cor. 5:20).

Having an exemplary character is essential if we want to mentor and develop other leaders. Just as Jesus served as an example for us to follow, we are to provide an example for our followers and those we are discipling. John Maxwell provides the analogy between a travel agent and a tour guide to highlight the contrast in leadership style. Some leaders, like travel agents, send people to places they themselves have not been. Servant leaders, on the other hand, are like tour guides who are able to say, 'Follow me, I know where I'm going because I've been here many times.'[18]

CHRISTIAN CHARACTER FORMATION IS AN ONGOING PROCESS THAT THE LORD CONTINUES THROUGHOUT OUR LIVES

Servant leaders open up space for others to follow – they don't send people out into the unknown. We journey together with those we are leading, and those being led gain confidence because they witness our exemplary conduct in the face of challenges, obstacles and opposition.

RESPECTFUL

I conducted a quick Google search of quotes relating to the word 'respect' and was surprised to see how many of them spoke of respect as being earned and not demanded. One example: 'You earn respect, so don't expect it from me straight away'. This contemporary view should be evaluated against the Bible. In Peter's first epistle he explains that Christians are 'foreigners and exiles' in this world, yet we are to 'live such good lives' so that people see our 'good deeds and glorify God'. He goes on to talk about submission to human authority as an expression of our freedom. Through our 'doing good' the criticism of the foolish will be silenced. He then concludes by saying, 'Show proper respect to everyone, love the family of believers, fear God, honour the emperor' (1 Pet. 2:11-17).

This is such a radical statement because of the context of the early church. They were living in a multi-faith culture, somewhere between Greek hedonism and Jewish legalism. They were subject to pagan Roman imperialism and emperor worship. They were living under the shadow of life-threatening persecution. In this hostile environment, many would expect Peter to call the believers to radical resistance – but instead he calls them to *submission*.

There's much more to say about this, but for our purposes we need to consider how this relates to Christian character – and particularly the character of leaders. Living in a hostile world, seeking to submit to God in our own context, and wanting to represent him well in the world, Peter calls us to 'show proper respect to everyone'. We are to show respect, whether we believe it is earned or not. We show respect to people because we are submitting to God and are motivated to do good deeds in order that God is glorified. Our goal as servant leaders should be to live lives that are beyond reproach. Ultimately, through being respectful to all people, we will earn their respect – even if given begrudgingly.

THE PROCESS OF CHARACTER FORMATION

These qualities of servant leaders do not emerge overnight. Christian character formation is an ongoing process that the Lord continues throughout our lives. God graciously leads us on a process that forms our character and matures us. Robert Clinton calls this the 'graduate school of life'.[19]

How does this happen? To my mind, there are three processes that God utilises in the graduate school of life through which he forms our character.

Devotion. The key way for us to grow in Christ-like character is to be fully devoted to God. When Jesus was asked which the greatest commandment is, he answered, 'Love the Lord your God with all your heart and with all your soul and with all your mind' (Matt. 22:37). As we focus our minds on Christ, seek to follow him, spend time with him, worship and adore him and seek to please him and represent him in the world, his character will be formed within us. It's a simple equation – the more devoted we are to spending time with Jesus, the more we will be transformed to become like him. Integrated in this process is devotion to the Bible as God's Word. Spending time reading, studying, memorising, hearing and meditating on the Word is absolutely essential if Christ's character is to be formed in us.

Difficulties. Another process God uses to form our character is the challenge of times of hardship, difficulty and persecution. Paul explains this process in Romans 5:1-5: he states that we can 'glory' in our sufferings because they lead us on a journey that produces perseverance, character and hope. Paul teaches us that there is a direct correlation between hardship and character development. This is not necessarily an easy pill to swallow. The key ingredient is perseverance. The reality is that Christian leaders will face difficulties, opposition, problems, failure and pain. Recognising that God can work in and through these situations in order to build our character is critical to choosing to persevere rather than quitting. Hebrews 11 summarises the faith journey of many Old Testament heroes of the faith and it is worth noting that all of these heroes were formed in God's graduate school of hard knocks. If we aspire to becoming Christ-centred servant leaders, then we will need to allow God to work in and through us during the difficult times to form us into the leaders he wants us to become.

Discipline. This is possibly even less popular than difficulties! The fact that God will discipline us can evoke resistance and even rebellion in our hearts. However, the Bible makes it clear that God disciplines us because he loves us and is working for our good. The process is most clearly explained in Hebrews 12:4-11 where the writer exhorts us to 'not make light of the Lord's discipline', going on to explain that although 'no discipline seems pleasant at the time, but painful... it produces a harvest of righteousness and peace for those who have been trained by it.' God disciplines us because he has a goal for us – that there should be a harvest of righteousness and peace. Therefore, unpleasant as we may experience it at the time, we must accept and embrace the Lord's discipline in order to fulfil our potential as leaders.

As I reflect on my own life, I can recall numerous occasions where God has revealed to me how far short of Christ's example my own character is. God has worked on my self-sufficiency through allowing me to go through a period of long-term illness where I learned to trust in his love for me, regardless of my ability to be productive in ministry. Through my devotional life, I am constantly made aware of the pride that quickly rears its ugly head and I continually need to recalibrate and humble myself through confessing sin. God has allowed my integrity to be tested when I had an opportunity to undermine those in authority over me in order to pursue my own ambitions. And I have learned that the process of God working on my self-sufficiency, pride and ambition (along with many other character flaws) is a continual process that

God graciously leads me through as I seek to submit to his lordship in every area of my life.

As we have seen, the process of character formation is not for the faint-hearted. It takes strength of character to become a Christ-centred servant leader in the 21st century.

CHAPTER 2

DEVELOP A PROPHETIC VISION

CHRIST-CENTRED SERVANT LEADERS HAVE A GOSPEL-FOCUSED VISION THAT CONTINUES GOD'S WORK ON EARTH

'It does not do to dwell on dreams and forget to live.' – Albus Dumbledore[20]

'Let your eyes look straight ahead; fix your gaze directly before you. Give careful thought to the paths for your feet and be steadfast in all your ways. Do not swerve to the right or the left; keep your foot from evil.' – Proverbs 4:25-27

In my first job as a youth pastor, as a green 22-year-old with limited theological training, I was privileged to serve under one of the most astute theologians and Bible teachers I've ever known. Our regular chats inspired me to understand scripture better and motivated me to dig deeper into God's Word.

One theological concept he introduced me to is the tension between 'the now' and 'the not yet.' We understand from the Bible that God's mission is to bring complete restoration to this broken world, which will ultimately be realised when Christ returns. That is the 'not yet' part – what we're looking forward to and yearning for. When we became Christians we were given a new identity as citizens of the kingdom of heaven with all the benefits of being God's sons and daughters, and yet we still live in a fallen and sinful world (2 Cor. 5:17-20). We are called to remain in the 'now' – as 'aliens and strangers', living our lives in a way that points people to God (1 Pet. 2:11). This is where the tension comes in. We understand that we ultimately do not belong here on earth, yet God calls us to continue to serve him as his representatives and ambassadors. We are called to be signposts for God – pointing people to the kingdom of heaven in our generation.

This is a good tension because it leads us to asking a critical question: how are we then to live? In particular, how do we live for God within our specific context and culture? It is important to understand that the Bible doesn't give an exhaustive answer to this question! The Bible does not give answers to every situational challenge that we will face in our lives or every contextual nuance of our generation. Rather, Jesus has given us his Holy Spirit who will teach us and guide us, never in contradiction to the Bible, as we seek to bring the kingdom of heaven to earth (John 15:15-18; 16:5-15).

This is the role and purpose of prophetic vision. Prophetic vision is derived from the tension of living in a fallen world, while also believing that God is at work in the world and engaging in human history to draw people to himself through Christ. Prophetic vision requires us to seek God for a picture of his ultimate intent for humanity, and then to discern how we should join the Holy Spirit in implementing it within our context. Jesus taught us to pray 'your kingdom come, your will be done on earth as it is in heaven' (Matt. 5:10). Prophetic vision pursues a picture of the kingdom of heaven, and seeks to bring that reality to earth. As Shane Claiborne has written, we then become the answers to our prayers as we seek to fulfil that vision within the generation and context that we live in.[21] So we can define prophetic vision as a picture of the kingdom of heaven that we seek to bring to reality in our present context.

> **WE CAN DEFINE PROPHETIC VISION AS A PICTURE OF THE KINGDOM OF HEAVEN THAT WE SEEK TO BRING TO REALITY**

Servant leaders serve their family, community, church, organisation and generation, by seeking God for a vision that will lead them to bring the tangible reality of the kingdom of God within their context. It is a requirement of servant leaders to inspire faith that this picture of the kingdom of heaven will become a reality in our present context.

The Message was born out of a prophetic vision of a picture of young people restored into relationship with God, of broken lives made whole, and of communities being transformed. This is the vision which still drives the organisation forward. In this we follow Christ whose own vision of the future was born in the Godhead before the foundation of the world.

I would argue that Jesus is the greatest prophetic visionary leader to have ever lived. Jesus' first recorded public message articulated his prophetic vision when he adopted the words of Isaiah 61 as his own personal mandate. Luke tells us that Jesus made his normal Sabbath day visit to the synagogue. He stood up to read and was handed a scroll from Isaiah's prophecy. Clearly, he sensed his heavenly Father's prompting as he read the passage and applied it directly to his own life and calling. He read the familiar words that the Messiah would bring good news to the poor and freedom to the oppressed... but then caused wonder and consternation by saying to them, 'Today this scripture is fulfilled in your hearing' (see Luke 4:16-21).

This passage defined for Jesus the big picture that he was working towards. He had a God-given vision that was derived directly from scripture. Throughout the gospels we see that Jesus wasn't operating arbitrarily or performing *ad hoc* good works. Rather, he had a specific plan as he worked towards fulfilling his prophetic vision.[22]

Jesus was bridging the 'not yet' and the 'now' because he had a cosmic vision of salvation that would rescue people and restore them into relationship with God. The incarnation of Christ was the fulfilment of a vision born in the Godhead – a vision of the salvation of humanity through the life, death and resurrection of Christ. This prophetic vision shaped all of Jesus' actions. That's why we can say that Jesus Christ is the greatest visionary leader who ever lived.

In Hebrews 12:1-3, we are given further insight as to how Christ's vision enabled him to complete his God-given assignment on earth. The writer states that, 'For the joy that was set before him he endured the cross, scorning its shame, and sat down at the right hand of the throne of God.' Jesus had a vision of the future, 'the joy set before him,' that enabled him to fulfil his calling even when he was despised, rejected, persecuted, beaten and ultimately killed. That is the power of a prophetic vision – it keeps us on course when the going gets tough. The author of Hebrews then instructs us to 'consider him' so that we will not lose heart. As we look to Jesus, we ourselves are given fresh vision and motivation to persevere in our own calling within the vision God has given us.

Vision is a destination that we know will be worth it in the end, even if the journey leads us through trial and hardship. Servant leaders should cultivate a prophetic vision because it will enable them to help their followers stay the course, persevere, and, ultimately, reap the rewards.

CULTIVATING A PROPHETIC VISION

Proverbs 28:19 is commonly cited when considering the subject of vision. It states: 'Where there is no vision, the people are unrestrained.' This could be interpreted as – without vision, people just do whatever they want. Prophetic vision enables us to see what God is doing and to lead people into obeying him. Vision is, therefore, a powerful force. Christ-centred servant leaders serve people by presenting a vision that enables them to see what God is doing in the world and how they can faithfully serve him. For every Christian, it's important to have a macro-level view of God's sovereign mission and recognise that our specific vision and calling falls within the cosmic scope of God's eternal plans.

The critical question each leader needs to ask is, how do I discern and cultivate a prophetic vision and contribution within the overall plans and purposes of God? As I've reflected on the example of the great men and women of faith in the Bible, it is clear that there is no single discernible formula or pattern of how they received their specific prophetic vision. God revealed himself in unique ways to biblical leaders and gave them a specific vision, or calling. Consider Abraham, Joseph, Moses, Gideon, Deborah,

David, Nehemiah, Isaiah, Mary, and Paul. Each of them had a prophetic vision with greatly varying ramifications in terms of the impact and outworking of the vision in their context. Therefore, it is important that we don't over-simplify the process of cultivating a prophetic vision, whether as an individual or as an entity. But there are some common threads that contribute to vision.

In my own life I can see how God has led me through a process of cultivating a prophetic vision which has increasingly come into sharp focus. I became a Christian as a child and felt a call to missions while I was still young. In my early twenties I became a youth pastor in Manchester. Through a casual conversation with my uncle (a pastor in South Africa), I felt prompted to move to Cape Town to continue youth ministry. As I began working with underprivileged youth in Cape Town, my heart was broken by the challenges they faced due to inequality and the legacy of apartheid. I used my passion for football to build relationships and mobilise mission into tough communities and prisons across Cape Town. Over the next few years this expanded as I had opportunities to travel across Africa and reach out to youth through football-based events. Through this opportunity, God began to stir in my heart a calling to invest in young African leaders as I saw they would be better equipped to reach their communities with the gospel. My heart again was stirred to provide a platform for emerging African leaders to flourish, particularly those who were marginalised. Through these circumstances, and many confirmations from scripture and other people, I began to sense a life-long vision. In 2011, I spent some time seeking God in

MY PERSONAL EXPERIENCE HAS BEEN THAT GOD HAS SHAPED AND REFINED VISION THROUGH A LIFE-LONG PROCESS

what I called a 'life-audit.' I read through years of journals in order to try and discern the thread of God's calling on my life. The result of that process was the emergence of a personal vision statement, which I summarised as being called to raise up African leaders to flourish in faith and life. In 2013, I joined The Message Trust and my personal vision aligned with the vision of the organisation I was joining, igniting passion in me to see God's kingdom come amongst gangsters and marginalised youth in order that they can become transformational leaders.

As God has taken me through this process over many years, I have found Isaiah 30:15 particularly helpful. The prophet writes, 'Whether you turn to the right or to the left, your ears will hear a voice behind you, saying, "This is the way; walk in it."' Prophetic vision can come into focus as we are walking forward in obedience to God. Sometimes we feel that vision will come in a flash of lightning or through some life-changing event. However, my personal experience has been that God has shaped and refined vision through a life-long process. Although I've had a sense of the big picture (and there is always the big picture of sharing the love of Jesus with those who don't know him), God has revealed more to me as I've sought to move forward with him. It may be different for you, but I do believe that part of the process of uncovering a kingdom vision is to keep on doing the things we know God has asked us to do. The more we do this, the more revelation he gives us.

Given that there is no fixed recipe for cultivating your vision, the remainder of this chapter provides insight into how to grow as a visionary leader through understanding four key elements that do seem to be consistent principles of discerning a prophetic vision.

To help us on this journey, we'll consider the example of Nehemiah as he cultivated a God-given vision.

FOUR STEPS TO DEVELOPING A PROPHETIC VISION

Step 1: Vision is God-given

Just as we have seen that there is a difference between secular and Christian leadership, so we should expect there to be a difference with regards to a secular and a Christian vision. Essentially, Christ-centred servant leaders should be seeking God for their vision. This not only changes the source of the vision, but also the scope of the vision.[23]

Nehemiah received a vision from God – a vision that was impossible to accomplish apart from God. He was a cup-bearer to a foreign king, living in a foreign land while his home country lay in ruins. What could he possibly hope to achieve? But God's vision seized his heart and led him on an incredible adventure. From the first chapter of the book of Nehemiah we can glean two key ingredients that will shape a God-sized vision.

Firstly, God stirred in Nehemiah a holy discontent (Neh. 1:4). Nehemiah heard a report from Jerusalem that rocked his world. Everything in him screamed, 'This is not right!' It was more than just a sad feeling, more than just a compassionate outburst – it was a holy discontent that changed the course of his life. Holy discontent emerges as a result of living in the tension between the 'not yet' and the 'now' we discussed above.

Vision is birthed and fuelled by holy discontent.[24] We can discover our vision by asking ourselves some key questions: what do we want to see changed in the world (either in our immediate situation, or in the place we live)? What wrecks your heart and bothers you the most? What causes you to say, 'I can't take this anymore – something must be done?' God leverages our discontent to provoke us to consider how he may use us to address the challenges. For some people it is a jaw-dropping, eye-popping moment (as it seemed for Nehemiah) that changes the course of our lives. For others, as it was with me, it is a nagging issue that stirs us over many years. So, discontent is always a mechanism for us to discover vision and to fuel us to action.

Secondly, Nehemiah's discontent led him to pray (e.g. 1:4,6,7,11). The opening chapter of Nehemiah is infused with Nehemiah's prayer as he takes his sense of injustice, and his urgent sense of calling, to God in prayer. His prayers were immediate and spontaneous – full of passion. He fasted and interceded for Israel. Through this insight into Nehemiah's prayers, we can recognise that he is looking to God for success (1:11; 2:20). By definition, vision should anticipate success. However, Christ-centred servant leaders will always recognise that success is directly proportionate to dependence upon God. Nehemiah was not afraid to ask God for success. But as he became successful, Nehemiah never forgot that God was the source of that success and therefore the one who deserved the credit. Remembering that our success is entirely dependent on the Lord is the antidote to the toxic danger of pride and causes us to remain on our knees in prayer.

Step 2: Develop a specific vision

In seeking God for our vision we should be asking for a specific vision – something that will make a tangible difference in the world.[25] Specific vision is developed by seeking to address explicit challenges with a detailed plan.

Nehemiah was addressing a specific challenge. He shared his vision statement to the Jews in Jerusalem: 'Come, let us rebuild the wall of Jerusalem, and we will no longer be a disgrace' (2:17b). His answer to the holy discontent he experienced was to mobilise the Jews to rebuild their city. This wasn't just a pragmatic response because he understood that God's reputation was at stake. In order to address the explicit challenge, Nehemiah developed a detailed plan (see 2:7-9 and 2:11-16). He conducted research, engaged the people in Jerusalem, and made sure he was prepared for the work ahead.

Developing a plan is both spiritual and practical. As we have seen, Nehemiah was a man of prayer and his plan was birthed in prayer.[26] Yet Nehemiah was also a practical man – he sought to understand the problems he faced and find practical solutions.[27] Christ-centred servant leaders will seek to find out for themselves the best way forward. This involves hard work, research, good communication and sometimes putting aside our own preconceived ideas. The result of this spiritual and practical work is a robust plan which helps mobilise people towards fulfilling the call that God has placed upon them.

Step 3: Count the cost

Cultivating a prophetic vision includes counting the cost. As far as is possible, we need to take full account of the implications of pursuing the vision.

Nehemiah knew what was at stake when he approached King Artaxerxes (2:2-3). Without the Lord's intervention, his very life could have been in danger as he was placing his future in the hands of the whims of a pagan king. Nehemiah had counted the cost and knew that risk-taking was part of the journey of faith that God was calling him to. Risky, courageous faith, is a necessary component of pursuing a prophetic vision. However, it is not risk-taking for daring's sake. It involves recognising that any great work for God will require steps of faith where we can't, humanly speaking, be certain of the outcome. But courageous vision compels us to be obedient to God, even if it appears this might result in great personal cost.

The cost for Nehemiah grew more intense as he continued to move forward with his vision (2:10, 19). Opposition and persecution became his daily reality, with his life constantly under threat. Against this opposition, he had to learn to persevere and continue in faith and wisdom.

Nehemiah 4 shows how he accomplished this: Nehemiah kept his focus on the vision, continued to speak in faith, maintained his vibrant prayer life, and mobilised his team for action. All great leaders have had to learn the art of perseverance if they are to accomplish great things for God. William Wilberforce, the great anti-slavery activist, wrote:

Each of us has a work to accomplish that has to do with our eternal well-being, a work to which we are naturally indisposed. We live in a world full of things that distract our attention and divert our efforts; a deadly enemy is always on hand to seduce and beguile us. If we persevere, then success is certain, but we must never stop trying. We are called to a life of continual resolution, self-denial, and activity.[28]

Wilberforce is right that we are 'naturally indisposed' to being Christ-centred servant leaders. Our human nature inclines us to a life of self-centredness and comfort. It will take perseverance to continue on the path of self-denial, carrying our cross, and pursuing the accomplishment of the vision which God has laid on our hearts – particularly in the face of opposition and persecution.

Yet, in spite of the risks and dangers associated with pursuing a prophetic vision, Christ-centred servant leaders can remain confident in God. Counting the cost is not to be a martyr or pessimist, but to have optimistic faith and confidence in God. Nehemiah boldly stated: 'The God of heaven will give us success. We his servants will start rebuilding' (2:20). If our vision has been birthed in God, then, as we count the cost, we can remain confident that he will bring us success.

Step 4: Communicate the vision

The final step in cultivating a prophetic vision is to communicate the vision to others. Visionary leaders need to share their vision. They are often compelled to share the vision. A true visionary leader will be constantly communicating the vision God has laid on their hearts. However, it is critical that leaders communicate vision in a way that inspires and enlists others, evoking passion within them to join the cause and work towards a better, Christ-centred, future. The Blackabys provide a cautionary note to a purely salesman approach to vision casting: 'Spiritual leaders don't sell vision; they share what God has revealed to them and trust that the Holy Spirit will confirm that same vision in the hearts of their people.'[29]

Nehemiah was a communicator *par excellence*. He ignited passion in his followers that caused them to accomplish a miraculous feat (2:17-18). Visionary leaders are passionate about what God has laid on their heart. The passion of Nehemiah flows from the pages. Passionate leaders are infectious leaders, inspiring faith and hope in those who hear them speak.

> **IT IS A DREAM SCENARIO FOR A VISIONARY LEADER TO SEE OTHER PEOPLE TAKE UP THEIR CAUSE WITH EQUAL PASSION AND ENERGY**

However, Nehemiah chose an appropriate time to go public with his vision. He also chose to share his vision with the appropriate people. Passion needs to go hand-in-hand with wisdom. Ultimately, the vision carrier needs to be the one that shares the vision. The outcome they seek is that those who hear the vision understand the core of the vision. A sign that a prophetic vision has been well communicated is that it ignites passion in others. Nehemiah effectively shared the vision with infectious passion – so much so that there was an immediate response from the people in Jerusalem. There was a collective response of 'Let's do this – we can do this!' It is a dream scenario for a visionary leader to see other people take up their cause with equal passion and energy... after all, a

God-sized vision will require a team of dedicated people to accomplish it. Prophetic vision passionately points people to God and invokes faith in him to believe that the impossible can become possible.

THE POWER OF STORY-TELLING

Communication doesn't stop when a vision is shared. Multiple opportunities need to be sought to share the vision, to encourage your team, and to provide focus. Successes must be celebrated and shared with great enthusiasm. Additionally, leaders can ignite passion by transferring the credit to others. Publicly affirming others is a powerful way to foster loyalty and passion in team members.

One effective way to communicate vision is to tell stories. Andy Hawthorne often says that The Message is a story-driven movement. We seek to share stories of God's goodness and faithfulness in as many ways as we can. In particular, we focus on transformational testimonies – demonstrating God's miraculous intervention in the lives of the urban heroes we raise up. We look for multiple media through which to tell the stories: in person, at churches, through newsletters, on social media, through podcasts, at prayer days, in our magazines and annual reports. As people hear the stories, it ignites faith and brings glory to God. In South Africa we have become so convinced of the importance of story-telling that we have a vision *to be a catalyst for new stories in South Africa through the gospel.*

Christ-centred servant leaders will continually serve their teams by communicating effectively, transparently and consistently – it is a core component of leadership and a skill which needs to be honed and developed over time.

Communication is all about motivation. In my years of being in leadership I have discovered there are two kinds of followers – those who are extrinsically motivated, and those who are intrinsically motivated; those who are motivated by external rewards and those who have an inner drive to complete tasks with excellence. In many organisations and companies, the best that a leader can hope for is that people are motivated because they have some stake in the outcome of the vision – perhaps a bonus or other such financial reward. They have passion that is dependent on a 'carrot' they are working towards. This is extrinsic motivation. Christ-centred servant leaders want to follow the example of Christ whose prophetic vision stirs up intrinsic motivation in his followers. For example, the disciples were not motivated by reward or personal gain. Rather, they had intrinsic motivation to pursue the vision of sharing the gospel, as is evidenced by the fact that they were willing to count the cost and lay down their lives. Intrinsically motivated people accomplish far more than those who are looking to get something out of it. A well-communicated prophetic vision by a humble servant leader can motivate and stir people to become intrinsically motivated – not because of the rhetoric or charisma of the leader, but because the Holy Spirit will stir them and align their hearts and passion to the prophetic vision that has been shared.

When I think of someone who God has used to stir vision and passion in me, I immediately think of the South African farmer, Angus Buchan – a man who has become a spiritual father to me and countless other people. From being a farmer who planted potatoes when everyone thought he was mad, to driving the Seed Sower gospel truck across Africa, to leading the Mighty Men movement, to calling a prayer meeting for over one million South Africans, he's a man whose holy discontent, ardent prayers, and mighty faith have driven forward his audacious gospel-centred vision. Angus Buchan has written:

> What I believe the Lord is saying is that without faith we can't please him and so we must not allow our vision, our dream to frighten us into failure. Let your vision be so big ... that if God does not do it, it is doomed to fail. Why do we say that? Because when it works God gets all the glory, people know that no man can do that.[30]

Grab a towel and let's follow the example of Angus Buchan and become Christ-centred servant leaders who pursue a picture of the kingdom of heaven and seek to bring it to reality in our particular context.

CHAPTER 3

MAINTAIN FAITHFUL STEWARDSHIP

CHRIST-CENTRED SERVANT LEADERS ARE FAITHFUL STEWARDS OF THE GOSPEL AND THEIR GIFTS IN THEIR GENERATION

'I am a custodian, my dear, not an owner. I must strive to be worthy of the task I've been set.' – Lord Grantham (Downton Abbey)[31]

'From everyone who has been given much, much will be demanded; and from the one who has been entrusted with much, much more will be asked.' – Luke 12:48

I have a confession. I occasionally watch British period dramas. I even enjoy them. Please don't judge me! But those wasted hours have provided me with a very helpful illustration for this chapter (the Lord works in mysterious ways!).

There is a scene in the popular British period drama, Downton Abbey, which provides a poignant analogy for what it means to be a Christ-centred servant leader. Lord Grantham, a member of the British aristocracy who inherited a large estate handed down to him through the generations, is talking to his eldest child, Lady Mary. According to custom, the inheritance – including land, title, and wealth – would only pass to the eldest male heir in the family (unfortunately our task here is not to discuss the unfairness of British patriarchy!) In explaining the situation to his grown-up daughter, Lord Grantham describes for her the role and function which has shaped his life and provided the lens through which he makes his decisions:

> If I'd made my own fortune and bought Downton for myself it should be yours without question, but I did not. My fortune is the work of others who laboured to build a great dynasty. Do I have the right to destroy their work or impoverish that dynasty? I am a custodian, my dear, not an owner. I must strive to be worthy of the task I've been set.[32]

As with Lord Grantham, we have received an inheritance we have not earned. It is the inheritance that Jesus Christ secured on the cross, and has been passed through the generations for 2,000 years. It is the inheritance of the gospel – a treasure beyond valuation. Each subsequent generation of Christians should recognise that they are custodians, not owners, of the gospel. They should strive to be worthy of the task that they have been set to enable them to pass on the treasure of the gospel to subsequent generations – having been faithful stewards of what was entrusted to their care.

In Peter's first letter he writes, 'Each of you should use whatever gift you have received to serve others, as faithful stewards of God's grace in its various forms' (1 Pet. 4:10-11). As Christ-centred servant leaders we are called to be 'faithful stewards' recognising that we have received an inheritance of which we are custodians, not owners, and of which we must one day give an account.

> **WE ARE TO 'TAKE SCRUPULOUS CARE' OF THAT WHICH HAS BEEN ENTRUSTED TO US**

I came across a phrase that provides a wonderful definition of what it means to be a steward: we are to 'take scrupulous care' of that which has been entrusted to us.[33] This is the *modus operandi* for Christ-centred servant leaders who understand their role as faithful stewards.

As a leader I recognise that I have a three-fold responsibility as a faithful steward. Firstly, I must take scrupulous care of the gospel. Our primary mandate is to be custodians of the gospel within our generation. Secondly, I must take scrupulous care of the vision which God has given me. As we saw in the previous chapter, God gives leaders a prophetic vision, and someday God will hold me to account for how I have stewarded mine in my tenure as a leader in The Message. And thirdly, God gives us gifts, talents and resources in order to fulfil our specific roles – for me, this is as a servant leader in the context of The Message. I must remind myself that I do not own those gifts, rather God has entrusted them to me so that I can faithfully serve him. As Albert Mohler puts it, 'The bottom line is this – we are merely stewards, not lords, of all that is put into our trust. The sovereignty of God puts us in our place, and that place is in God's service.'[34]

So how do we become faithful stewards? What do we need to understand about what has been entrusted to our care, and how we should strive to manage and conduct ourselves in a manner that ensures we are good and faithful stewards?

Jesus asked a similar question: 'And the Lord said, 'Who then is that faithful and wise steward, whom his master will make ruler over his household, to give them their portion of food in due season?'' (Luke 12:42, NKJV). He answered the question in terms of knowing and doing the will of the master. Therefore, to be faithful stewards, it is essential that we commit ourselves to knowing and doing God's will… to be faithful with what he has entrusted to us. Jesus helps us further understand this idea through a famous parable.

THE PARABLE OF THE TALENTS (MATTHEW 25:14-30)

Jesus gave this parable among a number of stories that he was using to describe the kingdom of God. His ministry on earth was nearing its end and he was providing his disciples with a perspective on the implications upon subsequent generations of his followers once he had returned to heaven.

In the story we see a wealthy man about to embark on a journey who entrusts his property, termed 'talents', to his servants. The owner was under no obligation to make this distribution. It was an act of grace intended for the good of the servants. The talents were a monetary amount and the three servants received different amounts. We are not told the reason for the differing amounts but the distribution was clearly at the owner's discretion and subject to his wisdom. The owner does not give specific instructions; the servants have liberty to choose how they use the talents (although, knowing their master, we can safely assume they should have known what he expected of them). Immediately, two of the servants put their talents to work and double the master's money. The third servant, however, digs a hole and hides the talent. Perhaps he was risk-averse. Maybe he was insecure. Or perhaps he simply didn't want to work hard and chose an easy option, thinking, 'Well, if I bury it, then I won't be tempted to spend it and can return it to my master when he returns.'

Upon the master's return, he calls his servants to give an account of how they have used the talents. The two servants who doubled their master's investment received high commendation as 'good and faithful' servants. But the servant who had no return on the master's investment is judged in the harshest terms. Jesus concludes with the stinging, 'For everyone who has will be given more, and he will have an abundance. Whoever does not have, even what he has will be taken from him.'

The implications for followers of Jesus are clear. God is the source of the gift, we are entrusted with his 'property' – his kingdom. The talents belong to him and he distributes them as he sees fit. The talents may represent many things (physical resources, our gifts and talents, our jobs, families, etc). Essentially, the talents represent the gospel and our responsibility as those who have received the gift of salvation. It is clear that our responsibility as servants and stewards is to invest what God has given us in order to realise a return for the kingdom. If we truly know Jesus, then we will know what is expected of us! Ultimately, we will be required to give an account for what we have received – an account to God himself. Indeed, the 'good and faithful' servants returned to the master the original investment plus the profit, thereby returning everything due the rightful owner as an offering.

The application of this is that if we have truly understood the gospel, we will present fruit back as an offering to God. Those who do not live fruitful and productive kingdom lives have, quite possibly, not truly understood the gospel in the first place, as they do not know the heart of their Lord.

Through this parable we once more see the counter-cultural nature of Christian leadership. Christian leaders are not looking for a selfish return on their investment into this life. Our goal is to please our master and be faithful with what he has entrusted to us. Our motivation is to be able to present to Jesus an offering of lives that have been impacted by the gospel on account of our labour. Our identity is that of a steward, recognising that we're called to a life of faithful obedience and service in order that we can also share in the Father's joy.

FIVE PILLARS OF FAITHFUL STEWARDS

Having established the correlation between servant leadership and stewardship, what are some of the practical implications for Christian leaders? In this section we discuss the example of Joshua – another biblical servant leader *par excellence* – and discover five pillars of a faithful steward.

MAINTAIN FAITHFUL STEWARDSHIP

Pillar 1: Kingdom succession (Joshua 1:1)

Joshua, following years of being discipled and mentored by Moses, is appointed by God to become the leader of the Israelites. God doesn't give him a specific title, but clearly the mantle of leadership is passed on to him as God says, 'Moses is dead... now you get these people ready to cross the Jordan.'

God is the ultimate succession planner! In his kingdom plan we must recognise that we are part of a bigger picture – that of God's sovereign plan that spans the ages of human history. As a Christian leader, we must always be cognisant of God's supreme purposes of which we are to play a part in our generation. Joshua understood this principle. The baton was passed on to him by Moses, and his responsibility was to steward God's people for the tenure of his life, before passing on the baton to the next generation. In the final chapter of Joshua (chapter 24), just before his own death, Joshua summons the people to Shechem in order to renew the covenant. He instructs the people, 'Now fear the Lord and serve him with all faithfulness' (24:14). Joshua recognised that his legacy was not simply going to be measured by his own faithfulness to God, but by whether the subsequent generation would also remain faithful to God.

The Apostle Paul had the same outlook. Towards the end of his life he wrote to his friend and disciple, Timothy. Paul was not only concerned with passing on the baton to Timothy... but through Timothy to subsequent generations of Christian leaders. He wrote, 'And the things you have heard me say in the presence of many witnesses entrust to reliable people who will also be qualified to teach others' (2 Tim. 2:2). Paul understood kingdom succession planning as he identifies four generations through which the baton must be passed:

Generation 1 – From Jesus to Paul

Generation 2 – From Paul to Timothy

Generation 3 – From Timothy to reliable people

Generation 4 – From reliable people to others

Once again we see that Christian leaders do not become 'owners' of the gospel or of the church, but are stewards. Therefore, we are part of God's kingdom succession planning and have a responsibility to the generations that will follow us. What we have received from a previous generation is not ours to alter, change, peddle for profit, or pervert in any way. It is not a leadership position we are entitled to. Rather it is a gift and responsibility that has been entrusted to us for that generation in which God has placed us. When Christian leaders fail in this task, the gospel is compromised and its effectiveness is diminished. The church loses its relevance and the light is extinguished to the detriment of all people in the world. The Bible is unambiguous about the call on Christ's disciples, and particularly upon leaders. Grab a towel because we are stewards of Jesus' legacy!

GRAB A TOWEL BECAUSE WE ARE STEWARDS OF JESUS' LEGACY

Pillar 2: Called by God (Joshua 1:1-4)

I can only imagine how Joshua must have felt when God commissioned and instructed him. In some ways it was maybe the fulfilment of a long journey in his life – from the moment he was chosen to be one of the spies sent into the Promised Land (Numbers 13). He had proved himself faithful over many years. Yet in other ways, this was just the beginning. He had seen the struggles Moses had had in leading the Israelites; now that responsibility fell on his shoulders. It must have been a daunting prospect. Therefore, this confirmation of his calling must have been extremely encouraging to him. This tangible encounter with God will have given him a strong foundation to face the challenges that lay ahead.

As we read scripture, we see that all of God's chosen leaders have a clear sense of calling – a commissioning moment. From Abraham to Gideon, David to Jeremiah, and from the 12 disciples to the Apostle Paul. Christian leaders have a clear sense of calling that comes through specific words, impressions and scriptures that God has graciously given them. This sense of calling is a gift of grace from God and has three key consequences for servant leaders who understand their role as a steward in God's kingdom.

Firstly, stewards recognise that the calling is always beyond them... and therefore they always need to depend on God. Watchman Nee says, 'God never asks us to do anything we can do. He asks us to live a life which we can never live and to do a work which we can never do...'[35] As with Joshua, the calling to be a steward in God's kingdom is always beyond us. This should force the Christian leader to remain dependent on God.

Secondly, steward leaders make their decisions based upon what God has said rather than on their circumstances. We are called to walk in obedience and faith. As we take steps of faith based upon God's instructions then we strengthen our faith muscles and are able to continue to take bigger and more daunting steps of faith.

And thirdly, steward leaders recognise it is always God's mission and ministry – never ours. God calls us to join him on his mission – that's the great adventure. And he always remains ultimately responsible for his mission. Christian leadership begins to get toxic when we start taking responsibility for something that is not ours. A warning sign is when we refer to 'my ministry', 'my organisation', 'my church' and even 'my calling.' Clearly this is not always wrong, but when it begins to usurp ownership of that which belongs to God, we are on very dangerous ground. Christ-centred servant leaders recognise that we've been called by God to be stewards and that our ministry and service is always primarily an act of worship to God.

Pillar 3: Heirs of the promises (Joshua 1:3-6)

The wonderful thing about God's succession planning is that leaders don't just inherit the responsibility to serve within the kingdom; they also inherit all the kingdom promises that God has given previous generations. God gives Joshua a succinct summary of all the promises he'd given Moses and then underlines that he's inherited these same promises by saying, 'As I was with Moses, so I will be with you; I will never leave you nor forsake you.' What a beautiful promise to receive at this critical point in his life. As it was for Joshua, so it is for us. We do not just inherit the kingdom mandate in our generation, but we also inherit all the very promises of Christ. This gives us confidence and assurance.

As Christian leaders we need to constantly remind ourselves of the promises we've received. We must regularly conduct an audit of our lives and leadership, and bring to remembrance all that God has promised us. This includes reminding ourselves of both the general promises that God has given all believers, and the specific and personal promises that God has given to us as individuals. This is why I'm such an advocate of keeping a journal. Whether a daily diary, or an occasional entry into a notebook, keeping a journal is an important tool to help us record the things that we believe God is saying to us. I find it incredibly helpful to regularly review my journals as a means of doing a 'system refresh.' Particularly during difficult and testing times, reflecting on God's promises is an incredible tonic that can boost our faith and strengthen us to remain faithful.

Pillar 4: Rooted in scripture (Joshua 1:7-8)

God underlines for Joshua that, in order to be a faithful steward, he needed to remain rooted in scripture. Indeed, he must meditate on it at all times. His success will be proportional to his commitment to God's Word. The Bible is the guidebook we need to live by if we want to lead as faithful stewards. Obedience to God's Word is the litmus test for our stewardship. 'Those who aspire to do anything for God and experience the richness he desires for them must be people of the Word!'[36]

Pillar 5: Redefine Success (Joshua 1:7-9)

God gives Joshua assurance of success. Having inherited the mantle of leadership, received God's specific call as an heir of God's promises and being rooted in scripture, Joshua can be certain of success. However, success is measured by his role as a steward in God's kingdom.

We touched briefly in the previous chapter on what it means to have a biblical view of success – and that visionary leaders recognise that success is in God's hands. Our responsibility is to be faithful to what God has called us to. God is ultimately responsible for the success of his mission. However, in a world that pursues success in terms of material gain and obtaining positions of power, how should we view success? How do we define success as we seek to fulfil God's calling on our lives?

John Wooden (1910-2010) was an extremely successful college basketball coach in the US. Among his many achievements as a coach, his UCLA team went on a seven-year winning streak of the NCAA championship. No other team has ever managed more than two successive championships. But more than his success on the court, Wooden is renowned for the philosophy he developed in order to bring out the best in his players. A major aspect of this philosophy was built upon his view of success, which he defined as follows:

> It is my feeling that real success is not the accumulation of material possessions or the attainment of a position of power or prestige. Rather, it is the peace of mind that is attained only by making the effort to do the best you are capable of doing at any task in which you are engaged.[37]

Wooden defined success in terms of giving our best effort. He didn't define it in terms of some specific outcome or result, but rather in terms of the 'peace of mind' that comes from the assurance of having done the best you could do. As Christian leaders, having 'peace of mind' is a great indicator that we are on the right track. We can leave the results to God.[38]

> **GOD IS ULTIMATELY RESPONSIBLE FOR THE SUCCESS OF HIS MISSION**

We can also consider success in terms of how well we have served others – have we truly given our best in the service of others? John Ashmen provides a great benchmark of success for Christ-centred servant leaders: 'In God's value system, success is not measured by how much we get but by how much we give.'[39]

POTENTIAL ROADBLOCKS TO FAITHFULNESS

Stewardship is a lifelong process of faithfully fulfilling what God has called us to do. The goal of the faithful steward is to please their master and hear those incredible words, 'Well done, good and faithful servant' (Matt. 25:23). But this isn't easy. Christian leadership is a marathon, not a sprint. I don't have to think hard to come up with stories of Christian leaders who ran well for a season, but ultimately stumbled and fell along the way – often bringing great damage to the kingdom. There are many potential roadblocks to being a faithful steward. The following are challenges that we have faced as The Message and that, I believe, are common barriers that leaders face to remaining faithful over the long haul.

Mission Drift. I can think of numerous organisations that were once at the cutting edge of mission but have seemingly lost their founding passion and calling. At The Message, we have unashamedly nailed our colours to the mast in our belief that true transformation only occurs as young people encounter and follow Jesus Christ. However, this is not a popular message in today's multi-faith, tolerant, postmodern age and we will always face the temptation to compromise in this area. As servant leaders, we are faithful stewards when we consistently avoid this temptation and seek to continually raise the temperature of mission within our organisation, which is fuelled by prayer. Mission drift can be a reality of any organisation that faces the daily pressures of sustainability within a rapidly changing world. Faithful stewards will always seek to 'keep the main thing the main thing' and not change course with every wind of opportunity. Christ-centred servant leaders will always acknowledge the primacy of the gospel, whether they are operating in business, church, government or non-profit leadership.

Show me the money. Financial pressure can bring about the temptation to pursue fundraising that distracts us from our core mission. Sometimes there are pots of money allocated to specific tasks which are not core to our vision. In the early 2000s there was a lot of funding available for HIV/AIDS education in Africa. Many organisations started an HIV programme because they were seeking funding. However, these programmes were not core to their mission and, in some cases, completely derailed those organisations. Another temptation is to accept money from donors who place restrictions on how the funds can be used – in particular, specifically requesting that funds not be used for Christian evangelism. At The Message, our position is that we will not accept money from anyone that restricts us from proclaiming the gospel. We believe that God will provide for the work he has called us to do... it's his vision, so he will provide in his way. This doesn't mean we only accept money from Christians, as God can provide in diverse and surprising ways. However, we will not let money dictate our agenda – that's God's job!

Believing the hype. Another threat to faithfulness is that we begin to believe the hype and think that we are somehow indispensable to God's plans. The outcome of this is pride in our success, and a quick path to unfaithfulness. We can begin to take on a 'superhero mentality' and think that we are the answer to the world's problems. A pastor friend once said to me, that graveyards are full of 'indispensable' people. God can use anyone for his kingdom purposes. Although celebrating success and sharing transformational stories is a wonderful thing, we must always remember that the success is not ours but God's, and that we cannot share in his glory. Rather, we are humbled that he allows us to serve him and others in his mission.

Becoming a Christ-centred servant leader means that we will be faithful stewards of the calling God has placed upon our lives. In particular, we are responsible to leave a gospel legacy, facilitating the continued expansion of the kingdom into future generations until Christ shall return. Christian leaders do not become 'owners' of the gospel or of the church. We all take our place in the roll call of Christ-followers who, for over 2000 years, have formed a grand procession, entrusted with the gospel message, proclaiming that Christ will one day return to call to him those who are his own.

The Bible is unambiguous regarding the call on Christ's disciples, and particularly upon leaders. We are stewards of Jesus' legacy, and it is the primary task of servant leaders to find trustworthy, reliable successors who are qualified to serve as stewards within their generation. I believe that Christ-centred servant leaders should be able to adapt what Lord Grantham said to Lady Mary and apply it to our responsibility as stewards:

> 'If I'd earned my own salvation and secured redemption for myself, I should be able to do with it what I choose, but I did not. My salvation, through the gospel, is the work of Jesus Christ who laboured and built a great dynasty. Do I have the right to destroy his work or impoverish that dynasty? I am a custodian, not an owner. I must strive to be worthy of the task I've been set.'

CHAPTER 4

BECOME DEEP WELLS

CHRIST-CENTRED SERVANT LEADERS CATALYSE OTHER LEADERS THROUGH GROWING IN MATURITY

Napoleon: 'I want my soldiers to march through the avenues of France in the shade.'

Berthier: 'Mon General, that will mean that we will need to grow trees and that will take 20 years.'

Napoleon: 'Exactement – that is why we must start today!'[40]

'...To equip his people for works of service, so that the body of Christ may be built up until we all reach unity in the faith and in the knowledge of the Son of God and become mature, attaining to the whole measure of the fullness of Christ.' – Ephesians 4:12-13

Imagine the scene: a backpacker ends up in a rural village somewhere in sub-Saharan Africa. For three days

83

he lives with a family in their simple hut, enjoying the truly indigenous experience. However, he is moved with compassion by the villagers' daily struggle for survival in the harsh and dry conditions. In particular, he notices the challenge that the women and children face each day as they hike a long distance to the nearest river to fill up their water jars – a daily task that takes over three hours to accomplish. He notes the wasted time for children who should be in school, and the physical strain upon the uncomplaining women. Humbled by the hospitality he has received, he determines that one day he will return and help the village.

Fast forward two years, and the backpacker has returned to Africa with a small team of committed activists. Since he was last there, he shared his experience with friends and family who all helped with fundraising. Moved by the photos of children dressed in rags and looking malnourished, they have raised significant funds. The backpacker made contact with an NGO and arranged for drilling machinery and the necessary infrastructure for a well to be dug near the village. Today, they 'turn on the tap' and the villagers dance and sing with joy as water flows freely. The children splash in the puddles, broad smiles on their faces delighting their international guests.

Over the next couple of years, the backpacker writes to the village on a regular basis. He is constantly reassured that the well has been a real blessing. Having told more friends about the project, he plans a return trip – this time to try and find a solution to the educational challenges that the children face. But as he approaches the village he is surprised to see women walking along the well-worn track towards the distant river, children in their wake, the scene evoking a sense of *déjà vu*. As he turns the final bend and the village comes into view, he sees his well – sand-swept and abandoned. His sadness turns to frustration and anger that his gift had been neglected.

Scenarios similar to this have been played out over decades in Africa as compassion-driven solutions have led to huge wastage of aid. As I have travelled extensively in Africa I've come to recognise that, in the face of the deep challenges, there are no quick-fix solutions to poverty and inequality. More could be said about how the backpacker could and should have genuinely empowered the village – but here I simply want to draw a parallel that introduces the leadership principle in this chapter. The backpacker made a shallow response to a complex situation that did not genuinely empower people. Just like donating a well that, without the training, support and resources to sustain it, will dry up and malfunction, so shallow leadership will not bring sustainable change to the lives of those they are seeking to serve. Becoming a Christ-centred servant leader means 'going deep.' In this chapter we will consider what it means to be a leader who is a deep well of resource who can serve people for the long haul and replicate that depth in the people they serve.

The term 'Urban Hero' was coined by The Message's Matt Wilson to describe the fruit that we are trusting will emerge from our ministry. Each year, our Urban Hero Awards celebrate stories of people who have turned from destructive and desperate lives and become productive people who contribute positively to society. We believe this transformation occurs as people have a deep encounter with Christ and embark on a journey of discipleship that leads to real transformation.

As Andy Hawthorne says, 'The only thing that Jesus is counting is disciples.' We are far more interested in those individuals who demonstrate the tangible fruit of their faith over a sustained period of time, than whether many people raise their hands in an initial response to the gospel at an event. Although that's important, it's just the first splash of faith. An 'Urban Hero' is a person who has undergone deep transformation over an extended period of time – someone who starts a ripple effect of transformation that impacts their family, friends, community and society at large.

OUR EFFECTIVENESS WILL BE DIRECTLY PROPORTIONAL TO THE DEPTH OF OUR RELATIONSHIP WITH CHRIST

We've discovered that, to see this happen, our leaders must be deep wells of resource, able to disciple people through the challenges, hardships and mess of life. Becoming a Christ-centred servant leader involves a commitment to going deeper because our effectiveness will be directly proportional to the depth of our relationship with Christ.

COMMISSIONED TO GO DEEPER

Paul gives leaders the following mandate in Ephesians 4:11-13...

> So Christ himself gave the apostles, the prophets, the
> evangelists, the pastors and teachers, to equip his people
> for works of service, so that the body of Christ may
> be built up until we all reach unity in the faith and in
> the knowledge of the Son of God and become mature,
> attaining to the whole measure of the fullness of Christ.

Sometimes referred to as the 'five-fold ministry', here Paul is high-lighting the different functions of church leaders. Whether one's primary gift is as an apostle, prophet, evangelist, pastor or teacher, each have the same primary objective: they are to work in harmony towards the goal of building up the body of Christ so that all God's people (themselves included) reach maturity, defined as 'attaining to the whole measure of the fullness of Christ.' It is those mature Christians who are then able to conduct works of service and themselves contribute to edifying the body of Christ. This is the ripple effect of kingdom ministry.

Just as Jesus commissioned the apostles to make disciples who obey all of Christ's commands (Matt. 28:18-20), so Paul is commissioning leaders to this primary purpose. We could conclude that the effectiveness of spiritual leaders should be judged by the maturity of those they are influencing. Robert Clinton says, 'Unless we experience God's ongoing development we will not be able to help others develop their leadership capacity.'[41] In other words, servant leaders need to be deep wells who are leading others to in turn become deep wells.

DEPTH IS PROPORTIONAL TO FRUITFULNESS

In Ezekiel 47, the prophet gives us an incredible vision of waters flowing from the temple of God. It is a beautiful picture that, in effect, depicts the temple as a reservoir of water that begins to flow out from the altar and move eastwards. The prophet measures the depth of the water which continues to deepen until it became a 'mighty river that no one could cross.' The water then flows to the Dead Sea and empties into the salty water, rendering it fresh. Suddenly new life emerges with vast quantities of fish. Trees grow on the banks and fruit is harvested. The vision concludes with the words, 'Their fruit will serve for food and their leaves for healing.'

There are many applications of this vision, one of which clearly shows the correlation between depth and fruitfulness. As the water flowed out from the presence of God in increasing quantity, as its depth increased and formed the powerful river, it resulted in tremendous fruitfulness – an abundance of life, food and healing.

Becoming a deep well leader is essential if we are to be fruitful leaders. The impact of our lives and ministry will be proportional to our depth, which in turn is proportional to us replenishing our well from the right source – the presence of God. The source of water in the Old Testament was depicted by the temple, the symbol of God's presence among his people. In the New Testament, Jesus is the source of blessing and the One who needs to be the source that fills our wells so that we can live fruitful and productive lives.

In John 4, we're introduced to a Samaritan woman, a known sinner with multiple marriages and in an adulterous relationship. She comes to Jacob's Well in Samaria to draw water. Because of her shame, she comes at an hour when no one else is around, and there she meets Jesus. He not only goes against the tradition of engaging in conversation with a woman, and against prejudice because she is a hated Samaritan, he also defies all reason and logic by revealing to this woman deep truths that would be repeated throughout history as some of the most profound words ever spoken. He reveals to this sinful Samaritan woman eternal truths that are foundational for all Christians who seek to become Christ-centred servant leaders. Imagine Jesus glancing at Jacob's Well as he spoke, 'Everyone who drinks this water will be thirsty again, but whoever drinks the water I give them will never thirst. Indeed, the water I give them will become a spring of water welling up to eternal life' (John 4:13–14).

The woman initially misunderstands Jesus, focusing on her need for physical water to quench her thirst. However, Jesus gives her keys to what he is to explain to others later in the gospel. Drawing spiritual nourishment from Jesus is critical to living life to the full (10:10) and bearing fruit that will last, fruit that will glorify God (15:4). Jesus is the source from which leaders must draw if they are to be deep wells. It is through him, and the gift of the Holy Spirit, that we are able to bear much fruit.

KEEPING THE WELL FULL

As I'm writing this chapter, Cape Town is in the midst of its worst drought for over 100 years. Every day we are given statistics on how our reservoirs are becoming depleted of their water reserves. The radio gives the bleak news that there is only 7% of usable water in the dams. If rain doesn't fall soon, then they will have to switch off the supply through the mains and water will no longer flow out of our taps.

All supplies of water need to be replenished with fresh water if they are to continue being a resource that sustains life. It's the same for servant leaders. We cannot simply give out all the time; our spiritual reserves need to be consistently replenished if we are to continue to be deep wells of resource, providing nourishment to those we are serving.

As we have seen, our ultimate source of refilling is to have a vibrant relationship with Jesus Christ. So what does this look like practically?

CONSERVE THE BALANCE BETWEEN *BEING* AND *DOING*

Twentieth-century pastor and author AW Tozer wrote that there is a tension in evangelical Christianity between 'being' and 'doing'. He wrote: 'Being has ceased to have much appeal for people and doing engages almost everyone's attention. Modern Christians lack symmetry; they know almost nothing about the inner life.'[42] Tozer claimed that the external activism of Christianity has taken over from the spiritual disciplines that connect us to Christ. Tozer is not advocating that one is better than the other, but that both are critical for a balanced and productive Christian life. Keeping our wells full requires that we maintain a balance between the spiritual disciplines of being in Christ, and our doing in his service.

As a young man, I learned the importance of the need for this symmetry. Having grown up in a Christian home, I made an adult commitment to Jesus when I was 17. At that point I became very involved in several service activities at our church. As an activist, I gained self-worth from feeling useful to God as I sought to please him with my dedication and hard work. However, when I was 19,

I fell ill with chronic fatigue syndrome. I spent three years highly incapacitated due to the levels of pain and exhaustion I experienced. For an activist, it was a really challenging time. I thought that God must have been frustrated with me as I could no longer do anything for him. One night I was lying awake and struggling with this, when I suddenly felt his presence with me in my room. I sensed his love, his grace, and his pleasure. I realised that his love for me was not conditional on what I could do for him, but was because I am his child. I recognised that my activity was therefore not a prerequisite to gaining his pleasure, but was an act of worship in response to his unconditional love. From that revelation, I realised that I should not seek to serve him unless I'm also depending upon him.

I'm still prone to be tempted to earn God's pleasure – and the only way to avoid that is to build a devotional rhythm into my life that causes me to ensure that I maintain the balance of being and doing. As someone said at a Prayer Day recently, it is like maintaining the balance between breathing in and breathing out. Both are required for life. We must breathe in – taking time in God's presence for worship, devotion, prayer, Bible reading, meditation, rest and relaxation. Jesus himself followed this cycle as he regularly took time out from the demands of ministry in order to be refreshed (for example, Matt. 14:23, Luke 6:12). It replenishes our wells and ensures we have the reserves we need to breathe out in acts of service. Each of us needs to consider how we avoid what Tozer calls the 'cult of commotion'[43] – the temptation to perpetual busyness that will inevitably drain our wells and leave us ineffective and unproductive as leaders.

Simply put, this is the instruction of Christ in John 15:4: 'Remain in me, and I will remain in you.' If we remain in Christ, we are then equipped to obey him (see John 14:15). The two go hand-in-hand: being and doing, remain and obey, worship and serve.

CONNECT WITH CHRISTIAN COMMUNITY

The Bible makes it clear that no Christian is an island. Just as servant leaders are modelling Christ-likeness to their followers, it is imperative that Christian leaders are part of a community of people who 'spur one another on to love and good deeds' (Heb. 10:24).

Being part of the community of a church is an essential way for Christian leaders to keep their wells full. Christian leaders should be part of a community that cares for them, encourages them, rebukes them, prays for them and motivates them. This kind of community energises leaders when they are feeling discouraged; it is a safe place where they can be vulnerable and open with others who they know are for them, not against them.

In Acts 2:42-47 and 4:32-35 we see how the early church developed Christian community. We see their unity, their care for each other and their devotion to the Word, to prayer, and to serving God in the city. It is important to note that the apostles were part of this loving and supporting community. As leaders, they knew that their fellow believers were praying for them, supporting them, and standing with them in both the good and the bad times. Christian community should serve as a refilling station for leaders. This could be in the form of a local church, small group, or among Christian friends in an accountability group. Depending upon your context, ensure that you have a group of believers who can 'speak the truth in love' to you (Eph. 4:15) and hold you accountable as a Christ-centred servant leader.

COMMIT TO BE SELF-DISCIPLINED

Paul loved to use imagery from the world of sport as a metaphor for the Christian life. In 1 Corinthians 9:24-27 he mentions athletics and boxing to highlight the 'strict training' that is required for success in the sporting arena. Likewise, he says, Christians need to exert great self-discipline in order to 'not be disqualified from the prize.' Self-discipline is a critical component of ensuring our wells are full. It requires self-discipline to maintain a vibrant devotional life and not just get caught up in busyness. It takes discipline to be part of a church community and to seek relationships that build into our life. Discipline is necessary in order to take care of our bodies so that we can stay 'in the race' for the long haul. Sometimes the hardest thing to do as a leader is to say 'no' when a seemingly great opportunity arises that will distract us from our core mission, or compromise our values. Jim Collins writes,

> True discipline requires the independence of mind to reject pressures to conform in ways incompatible with values, performance standards, and long-term aspirations... The only legitimate form of discipline is self-discipline, having the inner will to do whatever it takes to create a great outcome, no matter how difficult.[44]

It may appear counter-intuitive to say that self-discipline, something that seems hard to do, is something that fills our wells as servant leaders. Yet, the truth is, having poor self-discipline is a short-cut to emptying our wells and being distracted from our purpose.

CULTIVATE AN ENQUIRING MIND

One thing I have learned from my children is the joy of having an enquiring mind. My kids are naturally inquisitive and love learning. This was fuelled by my late wife who home-schooled them for many years. I feel that one of the greatest services I can do for them as a parent is to try to continue to fuel their love for learning.

Christ-centred servant leaders need to cultivate an enquiring mind that unceasingly seeks to learn and grow. Not only does this help us to expand our knowledge and understanding, it also helps keep us humble because, the more we learn, the more we discover what we don't know. It also helps us to appreciate other people who have expertise and knowledge in areas that we do not. Becoming a deep well leader means that we will 'maintain the attitude of a seeker,'[45] cultivating an enquiring mind that is not content with shallow thinking, generic clichés or platitudes when faced with the profound challenges of life.

God has created us to grow. Being a lifelong learner is an essential component of becoming (and remaining) a Christ-centred servant leader who is growing in their capacity to be a deep well and able to resource others. Many authors espouse the virtue of maintaining a posture of learning. John Wooden famously said,

'Learn as if you were to live forever; live as if you were to die tomorrow.'[46]

CONTINUE THROUGH SUFFERING

It might seem bizarre to say that suffering could be on our list of well-fillers. But it is not suffering *per se* that fills our wells – it is persevering in the midst of that suffering, particularly as we learn to trust in God and depend on him to bring us through the storm. It is as we go through the greatest tests that we learn the most about God, and become better leaders as a result. Suffering allows us to experience the faithfulness of God and build spiritual muscle which enables us to face the worst that the devil can throw at us, and to remain standing. Charles Spurgeon said, 'Whenever the Lord sets his servant to do extraordinary work, he will always give them extraordinary strength, or if he puts them to unusual suffering, he will give them unusual patience.'[47]

It is for this reason that we can rejoice in the face of suffering. As we persevere in him, our well of faith is filled. And the outcome of persevering through suffering is that we become men and women of faith who can aid others through their own times of crisis – a critical function of a deep well Christ-centred servant leader.

REMOVING BLOCKAGES

Just as we have reviewed ways in which our wells can be filled as leaders, we also need to be aware that our deep wells can become blocked and ineffective. Physical wells can be blocked up in numerous ways. They can be blocked by neglect, as sand blows in over time, muddying the water and filling up the shaft. Wells can be blocked by enemies who deliberately pollute the well by throwing in livestock that will rot and poison the water, or rocks that stop up the hole and prevent the water from being drawn out.

Christian leaders need to be aware of the potential blockages that can result from our own neglect or through allowing our spiritual enemy an opportunity to pollute or stop our effectiveness. We can also block our own wells with the rocks of sin and disobedience. Practically speaking, it is when we succumb to the inverse temptations of what it takes to keep our wells full, that we will block our wells and have our effectiveness as leaders diminished. Consider the following antitheses to the ways that our wells can be filled:

- Rather than conserving the balance between doing and being, many activist leaders can become workaholics. Driven by perfectionism, profit or applause, these leaders do not maintain the balanced cycle that is required to keep their wells full.
- Leaders who do not connect with Christian *community* can become isolated and independent. This temptation can result in a leader becoming unaccountable, negating the important early-warning processes that are fostered through Christ-centred community. Leaders can fall into many kinds of sin that block their wells and compromise their faith and testimony.
- Not committing to *self-discipline* can cause leaders to neglect to care for themselves in a God-honouring way. This can manifest in sleep deprivation, physical ailments, poor health

and addictive habits. A leader's well can become blocked because their integrity is compromised as there is no harmony between their words and actions.

- A leader who does not cultivate an *enquiring mind* will reach a plateau in their development as their well becomes blocked up by neglect of personal development.

All leaders will face challenges and hardships – both personally and in their ministry. It is part of the calling to leadership and should not come as a surprise to those who are called to become Christ-centred servant leaders. Those who do not continue through suffering will find that their wells get blocked with feelings of inadequacy and despondency.

MULTIPLYING DEEP WELL LEADERSHIP

The real purpose of being a deep well of resource is being able to invest in others who themselves will become deep wells. I think there are three principles that can help us become the kind of leaders who become multipliers of deep well leadership.

THE REAL PURPOSE OF BEING A DEEP WELL IS BEING ABLE TO INVEST IN OTHERS WHO THEMSELVES WILL BECOME DEEP WELLS

Firstly, as we have seen, we must start with ourselves. We need to go deep before we go wide. As we've seen many times with being a Christ-centred servant leader, this is contrary to much of current 21st century culture. There is a celebration of shallowness in the world as celebrities make a big splash today, but are gone tomorrow. It is also true of some

Christian evangelism which goes broad but has no depth. So we see thousands of people make decisions to follow Jesus but where there is no discipleship, a discouragingly high proportion of people fall away. The call of Christ is to make disciples. And the pattern he prescribed for us was to go deep before going wide, as Jesus himself instructed the apostles to start in Jerusalem, then Judea, then Samaria and then to the ends of the earth (Acts 1:8).

The Message Trust has always tried to follow this strategy. For 20 years, The Message focused on one city only – Manchester, England. Even when the World Wide Message Tribe was getting invitations to the four corners of the earth, they would never accept a gig if it conflicted with a schools-based outreach in Manchester. This investment over many years has not only had a deep impact on the spiritual vitality of the city, but it has also given the Manchester hub office a depth of resource and experience that now undergirds the global movement.

What holds true for organisational development is also true of personal ministry, for discipleship and for leadership development. This is then the second principle – it is a long-term investment if we want to develop deep-well leaders who will become a rich resource for others. Just as this chapter opened with the story of a well in an African village that was ill-equipped to sustain the community long-term, so too will it take careful preparation, planning and an intentional process in order to lead people to maturity in Christ. There is a reason that Paul told Timothy not to be hasty in laying hands on new believers for leadership positions (1 Tim. 5:22) – he knew that they needed to travel a long road, often in the school of hard knocks, before they would be ready. In other words, Paul knew they needed to go deep before they could go broad.

The third principle is that deep-well leaders need to see the big picture. There are no shortcuts to multiplying leaders. Deep-well leaders recognise that raising up other leaders is a lengthy process, but the end result is a leader of substance – like an oak tree – able to stand firm for God and be a blessing to many. A deep-well leader realises that, if nurtured correctly, every acorn has the potential to become a forest of oak trees, so it is worth taking time, having patience, and keeping the big picture in perspective.

With leaders like that, God can bring transformation to broken people and communities around the world.

CHAPTER 5

PUT PEOPLE FIRST

CHRIST-CENTRED SERVANT LEADERS PUT PEOPLE BEFORE PROGRAMMES, PROJECTS AND PROFIT

'Submit to one another out of reverence for Christ.' – Ephesians 5:21

'It's amazing how much can be accomplished when no one cares who gets the credit.' – John Wooden[48]

I remember an early experience I had with The Message where one of the leaders from the UK, who I didn't know that well, had gone above and beyond the call of duty in order to show me support in my new role. When I Skyped him and thanked him for what he'd done, he simply said, 'Hey, we're family!' That spoke volumes to me of the level of commitment that people within the organisation had towards one another, and my loyalty to the organisation increased exponentially because I felt loved and cared for.

The relational dynamic in organisations like The Message can be a fascinating phenomenon. Consider the team I lead in South Africa. We are a diverse bunch to say the least! We range in age from 20 to 70. We range in education level from no school-leaver's certificate to PhD graduates. We are from diverse cultural and language backgrounds. Many of the team have spent time in prison, while others come from considerable privilege. Inevitably, the team has a vast array of life experience, talents and theological background. What brings such a 'Liquorice Allsorts' bunch of people together?[49]

Initially, for most of the team, they joined The Message because they believe in the mission of the organisation and felt that they have a contribution they can make. What brought us together was a sense of purpose. However, when working together in close proximity over a long period of time, the mission and purpose of the organisation is not sufficient to maintain unity when conflict arises. Ultimately, what will keep my team committed to the mission, to me and to one another, is if they know that they are valued as individuals.

THE ONLY WAY TO MAINTAIN UNITY IN DIVERSITY OVER THE LONG HAUL IS TO PUT PEOPLE FIRST

Andy Hawthorne has coined the quintessentially British phrase 'We're Mates on a Mission' to express what we're trying to accomplish at The Message. It's the mission that brings us together – but it is bonds of love and friendship that will keep us together through the ups and downs of ministry. That's why the hallmark of leadership presented in this chapter is so critical for Christ-centred servant leaders in the 21st century. The only way to maintain unity in diversity over the long haul is to put people first.

'I HAVE CALLED YOU FRIENDS'

When Jesus grabbed a towel and washed his disciples' feet, he was expressing an act of love that embodied the attitude of servant leadership he had demonstrated throughout his three-year period of public ministry. Jesus invested in people. He put people first. It infused everything he did. This is particularly evident in the investment he made into those closest to him.

His twelve closest followers were from diverse backgrounds and had different strengths and weaknesses. He invested in their lives over three years, teaching, encouraging, supporting, rebuking and loving them. They not only shared in his public ministry, but he took them aside privately to give them extra instruction and insight. He entrusted them with responsibility, although he never sent them out alone – but sent them out in pairs, debriefing them when they returned. The Twelve had unlimited access to Jesus who 'did life' with them. Although, initially, the disciples made countless mistakes, were beset with infighting and competition, and at one point abandoned Jesus completely, eleven of the Twelve ultimately went on to change the world and cause a ripple effect that still reverberates around the globe today.

What was Jesus' secret to fostering unity in diversity to ensure long-term impact? Obviously, he was the Son of God who had experienced the perfect unity of the Godhead since before the dawn of creation – you might suggest that that gave him a 'competitive advantage' when investing in people! However, being the Son of God surely could have had the opposite effect because we could argue that he didn't need to invest in others. Rather, he chose the difficult task of limiting his own powers in order to train and mobilise the disciples. In doing so, he modelled for all future

Christian leaders the essence of collaborative servant leadership. I would suggest that Jesus was the architect of what I highlighted above – Jesus understood the concept of being mates on a mission. Consider what he said:

> I no longer call you servants, because a servant does not know his master's business. Instead, I have called you friends [mates!], for everything that I learned from my Father I have made known to you. You did not choose me, but I chose you and appointed you to go and bear fruit – fruit that will last... This is my command: Love each other. (John 15:15-17).

Jesus empowered his disciples, and all his followers for all time, to exemplify this kind of commitment to each other through the gift of the Holy Spirit. In fact, receiving the Holy Spirit was a game-changing moment for the disciples, which enabled them to invest in others as Christ had invested in them.

The good news is that the Holy Spirit is still the empowering personality that enables 21st century servant leaders to love people with the love of Christ. Christ-centred servant leaders follow Jesus' example and put people first – prioritising relationships over projects, programmes or profit. In order to do so, they will be committed to friendship and love... in other words, they will be mates on a mission who understand the power of putting people first.

AN UN-SEXY WORD

Becoming Christ-centred servant leaders requires a total commitment to the people that we have the privilege to lead. Following Paul's instruction in Ephesians 5:21, we recognise that this goal will only be achieved if we 'submit to one another out of reverence for Christ.' Submission is not a common theme in secular leadership material so probably needs a little explanation.

Submission doesn't imply being a doormat that anyone can walk over. Submission is also not weak leadership but means having the strength of character to be willing to set aside our own ideas, ambition and pride for the good of others. The key to fostering an environment of mutual submission is genuinely having a high view of other people. Paul gives us this key in Philippians 2:3 – he says that 'in humility consider others better than yourselves.' Christ-centred servant leaders are prepared to submit to those they lead because they see them as better than themselves.

The antithesis of this approach is self-serving leadership that result in toxic organisations. Self-serving leaders put their own agendas first, and they always put the interests of the organisation or project before the interests of their team. They often lead through fear, ensuring that their subordinates submit to their desires and whims, while also guaranteeing there is a scapegoat should anything go wrong. Many companies, corporations and even Christian organisations and churches are built in this way. This kind of toxic environment breaks down trust and feeds upon unhealthy competitiveness which fuels the fixation on the 'corporate ladder' – the goal of which is to climb as high as you can regardless of whether you do so at the expense of others along the way. Those at the top of the ladder are clearly the most 'important' who need to keep their subordinates in submission to them in order to protect their status and their perks.

Christ-centred leaders who grab a towel in order to serve people are of a different ilk altogether. People are the priority of Christ-centred servant leaders. However, it is not always easy to cultivate an environment that puts people first – particularly in the context of our highly individualistic and self-absorbed society. So how does this work practically? How can we cultivate an environment that puts people first? How do we become the kind of Christ-centred servant leaders that can build a great organisation without compromising in this area?

This is an area where I've experienced both success and failure. As a highly driven, goal-oriented person, I'm sure there are people who have worked with me who could point the finger at times when they haven't felt like they were at the top of my list of priorities. I confess that sometimes I've put the interests of the organisation before the people who worked for the organisation. Out of the pain of these experiences, I have learned that we need to focus on *togetherness*, *teamwork* and *trust* in order to cultivate an environment which genuinely puts people first.

TOGETHERNESS: THE POWER OF UNITY

Unity is a constant theme of the Bible, from Genesis to Revelation. In Genesis 1, we are introduced to the unity of the Godhead, Father, Son and Spirit, who said 'Let us make man in our own image' (v.26). The togetherness of the Trinity is revealed throughout scripture, and beautifully depicted at Jesus' baptism. As the son is baptised, the Father declares his love and affirmation from heaven, while the Spirit descends upon him in the form of a dove (Matt. 3:13-17). The Godhead are perfectly united in their mission to restore the broken relationship with humanity.

Human beings intimately reflect the Godhead when we live in unity. From when God said 'it is not good for man to be alone' (Gen. 2:18), through to John's vision in Revelation, in which he sees heaven containing a great multitude of people 'from every nation, tribe, people and language', united in one voice as they worship God (7:9-11), God has intended for human beings to be united. However, the scourge of sin and evil has completely derailed God's intentions, and human history is littered with division expressed through wars, racism, genocide and hatred. In contrast to this, Christ-centred servant leaders are called to lead people towards togetherness, through love expressed in unity and equality.[50]

Servant leaders need to remember that people are their greatest asset, and promoting togetherness unlocks incredible potential that can drive an organisation to accomplish results that exceed all expectations. Love is the key to togetherness. Perfect love has existed in the Trinity before the dawn of time, and the Trinity will continue to be united in love for all eternity. Becoming a Christ-centred servant leader will mean we love others as Christ loved us (John 15:12). As Peter instructs, we must 'love each other deeply, because love covers over a multitude of sins' (1 Pet. 4:8). Love is required if we are to grab a towel and serve people as we seek to build up, to affirm, to honour, to bless and to respect those we are leading.

Fostering togetherness can be particularly difficult as an organisation grows. Typically, a small organisation, company or church in its founding phase is characterised by a strong sense of calling and a tight relational bond between the founders. In this phase, everybody knows everything that's going on and there can be a Musketeer-like commitment to 'all for one and one for all.' But as an organisation grows and becomes more structured and institutionalised, it can be easy for people to drift from the sense of togetherness that defined them in the early years.

This is why it is important that the founding culture of an organisation is defined and regularly shared. New team members need to be oriented into 'the way we do things here.' These are often presented as the values of the organisation. However, if there is disconnect between the stated values and what a staff member actually experiences, then this undermines unity. I have learned that it is imperative that leaders conduct a form of 'values audit', evaluating if the values that they hold so dearly are actually being absorbed into the lifeblood of the people in the organisation. The founding or longest-serving team leaders need to be involved in consistently reviewing and discussing the values with the team. This helps foster unity and is a clear way of prioritising people over programmes, projects and profit.

Christ-centred servant leaders will also foster togetherness through simple acts of love conducted on a daily basis. These can include: asking people how they are – and waiting for an answer. Congratulating staff for a job well done. Being kind. Sending notes of encouragement. Trying to remember birthdays, anniversaries and other important events in the life of your team members. Sometimes discipline and correction is required. However, if people know that you are ultimately for them and not against them, even correction can be received as a form of love and contribute towards unity. If we grab a towel and set the example in these things, others will follow. Who wouldn't thrive in that kind of environment?

TEAMWORK: IT DOES MAKE THE DREAM WORK

My Message South Africa colleague Mark Slessenger likes to use the illustration of a soccer formation to demonstrate the importance of teamwork in the organisation. In a soccer formation, every player is committed to one thing – to score a goal and win the match. In order to do this, it is imperative that each player knows and understands their position, and performs in that position to the best of their ability in order to serve the team and help them achieve their common goal. When defending a corner, the best headers of the ball will come and mark the tall strikers from the opposition. If a person wins a penalty, it is not necessarily their job to take the resulting penalty kick, but rather the specialist and pre-chosen penalty kick-taker will step up in order to maximise the chance to score the goal. Playing to our strengths is an act of service that helps the team perform at the highest level.

The other powerful aspect of this metaphor was highlighted to me through a conversation I had with a friend who used to play for Manchester United. He told me that, even at that level, players realise that not everyone performs to their full potential in every match. In fact, in most games, even in a great team, three or four of the players may be having an 'off day.' But it's important that the players who are on top of their game step up and 'have the backs' of their teammates in order that the team as a whole is still successful. One motivation for this is that the players on top of their game in one game will know that their off day may be round the corner, and they'll need their team members to step up and assist them at that point. A team that operates in this kind of spirit – whether in soccer, business, or ministry – can accomplish great things. This reminds me of King Solomon's principle that two are better than one because they'll have a better return for their effort. And if one falls or is struggling, they can rely on their teammate to help them up again (Eccl. 4:9-12).

It can be easy to extol the value of teamwork, but it's far harder in practice to build a great team. Sometimes it seems easier to go it alone – there is less conflict and it may appear quicker to get tasks done. However, this is short-sighted and self-serving leadership. As John Maxwell says, 'One is too small a number to achieve greatness.'[51] I have learned that, in order to build great teams, then our team members need to feel valued and be operating in their areas of gifting and passion. When this happens, dynamic and productive energy can flow that enables everyone to accomplish exceptional results. But, in order to reach that point, Christ-centred servant leaders will value their team members as of highest importance.

There is an approach to leadership that advocates that 'leader knows best', and his or her job is simply to make sure that they lead their team in such a way that everyone buys in to what has already been determined by the leader. The goal of leadership ultimately becomes to manipulate people, by whatever means necessary, to conform to the leader's predetermined agenda.

This cannot be true if we want to become Christ-centred servant leaders. Although leaders will undoubtedly have opinions and ideas as to the way forward or how to resolve a particular issue, Christ-centred servant leaders genuinely welcome the opinion of other members of their team. Compliance to a leader who continually pushes their own agenda does not build strong teams – even if there is the appearance of productivity and progress.

Servant leaders will not only invite discussion and feedback, they will also be willing to change their mind, alter course, and implement new ideas that come from their team. In this way, team members realise that their input really matters and that their opinion can sway strategy and contribute to positive outcomes. Stephen van Rhyn, pastor of Jubilee Community Church in Cape Town, has this approach in leading his church. Simply put, he says, 'The best idea in the room wins,' even if this idea comes from the most junior or 'unqualified' person. After all, a Christ-centred servant leader is looking for God's leadership and knows that God can speak through any person at any time (as demonstrated countless times in scripture, most notably when he spoke through a 'dumb ass').

Additionally, godly teams ideally need to have a representation of people from different backgrounds who have different life experience and are from diverse cultures. This must be more than mere 'window dressing' – there needs to be a commitment to pursue diversity and ensure that everyone's voice gets heard.

It is easy to build teams of people that look, think and behave like us. However, those teams lack depth and flavour – they can quickly become stale and irrelevant. It may be more difficult to build multicultural teams of people who look, think and behave differently from us. Christ-centred servant leaders recognise that their worldview is limited and shaped by certain perspectives related to their cultural heritage. To truly grow as leaders, we need to expand, or even explode, our narrow worldview by embarking on a journey of discovery with people who have a different perspective. This makes life richer, and enables us to become better leaders.

TO TRULY GROW AS LEADERS, WE NEED TO JOURNEY WITH PEOPLE WHO HAVE A DIFFERENT PERSPECTIVE

Evidence that a strong team exists is that the principle of 'Rotating functional leadership' can occur.[52] This flows from an understanding of how Team Trinity operates. The members of the Godhead have different functions as Father, Son and Holy Spirit. As the biblical story unfolds, we see mutual submission displayed in the Godhead as each member defers to the other. Jesus defers to the Father throughout his life on Earth, and the Father glorifies the Son as he demonstrates obedience. Then, as the Holy Spirit is poured out at Pentecost, we see a new era introduced as had been prophesied by Joel 2:28-29, as the role of the Holy Spirit comes to the fore. As for Team Trinity, so for us. Rinehart explains it this way: 'We practise mutual submission and are quick to defer to one another... Each person has a function, and when that function is needed, that person becomes our leader.'[53]

The key to practising rotating functional leadership is to genu-inely value one another and recognise that God has called our team members to be part of our team because they offer something unique to the team that we do not. And when their gifts are called for, we submit to their leadership. Rinehart goes on to explain: 'Each believer can be a leader in the arena of his or her particular gifting. Conversely, every believer and leader is a follower as well. This happens when believers defer to one another in the areas of their gifts.'[54]

TRUST: THE MOST POWERFUL MOTIVATION FOR TEAMS

If we want to build teams that work together, we need to foster an environment of trust, built upon the foundation of a godly character as we discussed in Chapter 1. Characterless leaders never engender trust, and unity will never result where there is no trust. Rather, 'Character is the place where one's deep hunger, personal identity, and calling merge to generate the confidence that allows people to trust a leader and agree to journey together.'[55] Trust is therefore the most powerful motivation for teams that work together.

Yet trust seems to be a rare component in many teams. Rather than building trust, many leaders erode trust over time and have to resort to other means in order to

TRUST IS THE MOST POWERFUL MOTIVATION FOR TEAMS THAT WORK TOGETHER

persuade or manipulate people to perform. I have experienced the negative and toxic corrosion of trust which results from everyone looking out for their own interests rather than for the common good. Trust is corroded when the leader does not put people first, but uses people to his or her own ends. Trust is corroded over time as leaders make consistently bad decisions, undervalue their people, and expect them to perform without giving them the support or resources that they need. Trust is corroded when people feel unappreciated, when the leader takes all the credit and when the truth is compromised.

This being the case, what can we do to build trust in order to foster togetherness and teamwork?[56]

Seek to understand the individuals on your team. Leaders are often portrayed as solution-based people who are constantly juggling multiple balls and seeking to maximise every moment of every day to accomplish as much as possible. If that is the paradigm of leadership that you've subscribed to, then you are going to find this aspect of trust-building very difficult, because seeking to understand individuals on your team involves time and listening.

Some of the most impactful leaders I've encountered were not actually super-energised, Duracell Bunny, Red Bull-guzzling types. They were instead those who took the time to get to know me, find out about me, and show genuine interest... they listened. They were prepared to keep their phone in their pocket, turn away from their laptop screen and not always order coffee to go. It was these people who gave me the best advice. They didn't just reel off clichés or platitudes, jump to solutions, or interpret everything I said through their own perspective or experiences. No, they took time to prayerfully consider what I was saying, gave measured responses, and treated me as an individual. This kind of person I am happy to trust – because I know they are interested in me. Genuinely seeking to understand our team involves the discipline of listening – and that is probably going to impact your diary. Yet it is essential if we want to be trusted by our team members. We need to rediscover the lost art of listening.

Attend to the little things. Married couples know that minor issues can cause major conflict if they go unresolved. Conflict is often about the little things – the ongoing irritations of doing life with someone who continues in their annoying habits even though we've graciously asked them not to do it time and again. The little things build up – to become big things!

When I was an engineering apprentice I had the opportunity to work on the Channel Tunnel project. This included some site visits to Calais to work on the French side of the tunnel. I was based in a Portakabin office and my colleague and I would get to work early to maximise our days. Once settled at my computer and trying to focus on my work, I would then be interrupted every five minutes as each French colleague who came to work that morning would go round the entire office and shake everybody's hands. At the time I found it amusing (and a little irritating) – it wasn't something we did at our corporate office in Manchester. But it is a habit I've since adopted, and now at The Message, I try and go round the office and greet everyone every day – shake their hands (or high five or hug, whatever you're comfortable with), look each person in the eye, and say 'good morning.' It's a little thing – but it reminds me that people are my priority, and hopefully is a little thing that makes my team feel valued.

Attending to the little things can include noticing when someone has done a good job and affirming them in it. Angus Buchan has written: 'If you want those in your charge to reach great heights, it's not going to be through extra lessons or extra coaching, but through affirmation.'[57] It includes saying 'please' when we ask people to do something for us, and 'thank you' when a task is accomplished.

Keep commitments. This can seem obvious, but is often overlooked. If you have committed to doing something like attending a meeting, sending a report in on time or helping with a practical task, then make sure you do what you've promised to do. And, if for some reason you can't do it, then let the person know well in advance – value them enough to tell them. Not keeping commitments is a major 'account withdrawal' and people who consistently do not keep commitments will lose the trust and confidence of their team.

Some leaders have the tendency to be people-pleasers. It is not a bad thing to want to try and make people happy. However, the danger with being a people-pleaser is that it's very easy to make promises you can't keep. An important principle of being a Christ-centred servant leader is not to over-promise and under-deliver. If there is any doubt, then rather 'under-promise' in order that you can 'over-deliver'. Then, if you over-deliver, you have built trust and people's confidence in you will grow.

Clarify expectations. Trust is hard to build without clear expectations, in other words when your team doesn't understand where they are going or what is expected of them. Leaders who constantly move goalposts will find that their teams lose trust in them as ambiguity will undermine confidence. Leaders need to provide clarity on the direction in which the team is moving, and the role that each team member will play. Practically, this is why aspects such as job descriptions, annual reviews and performance appraisals are useful tools in the leader's kit. Additionally, having clearly defined goals that everyone agrees on and works toward will provide focus and clarity.

SIMPLY PUT, TELL THE TRUTH! KEEP YOUR WORD! DON'T LIE! MAINTAIN INTEGRITY

Showing personal integrity. An environment of trust is directly proportional to the level of integrity that a leader displays. 'The trust others have in us depends on our level of integrity. Integrity is essential to trust. It elicits trust.'[58] As we saw in Chapter 1, integrity is ensuring there is consistency between our words and actions. If we are inconsistent, then those closest to us, our team members, will pick up on it before anyone else. Once our integrity is compromised, then it becomes almost impossible to regain the trust and confidence of your team members. Integrity involves telling the truth. It sounds easy, but it's so simple to bend the truth, tell so-called 'white lies', exaggerate and downright mislead people. Billy Joel sang that 'Honesty is such a lonely word', but it is an essential word for Christ-centred servant leaders. Simply put, tell the truth! Keep your word! Don't lie! Maintain integrity.

Apologising sincerely. There is a school of thought which believes that to admit mistakes is a sign of weakness. This is a misguided belief. Leaders who never admit their mistakes will not build trust. Additionally, when our mistakes have directly offended, let down, or hurt someone on our team, Christ-centred servant leaders must apologise. And the sooner the apology follows the offence, the sooner trust can be restored. The Bible underlines that Christian community includes the discipline of confession – specifically, confessing our sins to one another (Jas. 5:16) with the instruction that we must also forgive one another because Jesus Christ forgave us (Col. 3:13). The discipline of confession seems to have been eroded in recent times, with Christians feeling a pressure to present their best selves to one another, rather than their weaknesses. However, being vulnerable enough to admit our failings and apologising for mistakes takes away the mystique of leadership and allows people to see that leaders are ordinary people who are not infallible.

For Christian leaders, these principles need to flow from our commitment to other believers in church and into every environment in which we operate. Having the humility to admit our fallibility and apologise to those we have offended (whether believers or not) is evidence that the Spirit of Christ is genuinely at work within us. Yet change must follow repentance. If leaders continue to make the same mistakes and give token apologies, then this insincerity will result in diminishing trust. So when we recognise we've made a mistake, we need to timeously correct matters to ensure that it doesn't happen again. That is true repentance.

THE KEY INGREDIENT

You will probably have noted a common thread in this chapter that is essential if we are going to put people first – it can be summed up in three words: communicate, communicate, communicate! Perhaps it is possible to over-communicate, but a Christ-centred servant leader will never be able to demonstrate their commitment to people if they under-communicate.

Cultivating a united team, built on a foundation of trust, is dependent upon communication. Rather over-communicate than risk the potential uncertainty and ambiguity that may accompany under-communicating. Ultimately, as leaders grab a towel and seek to serve, we are communicating that we value those we lead and that we are putting people before programmes, projects and profit.

GIVE POWER AWAY

CHRIST-CENTRED SERVANT LEADERS EMPOWER OTHERS TO FULFIL THEIR POTENTIAL

'To do for others what they have the capacity to do for themselves is to disempower them.' – Robert Lupton[59]

'Go in the strength you have and save Israel out of Midian's hand. Am I not sending you?' – Judges 6:14

Our Message South Africa COO, Mark Slessenger, speaks of the need for leaders to have a kingdom ripple effect. The image is of a stone being dropped into the centre of a pool of water and causing ripples that move in concentric circles right across the pool until they lap the sides. So, as we empower young people, they will cause a kingdom ripple effect in their families, communities, neighbourhoods, city and country. For this to happen, genuine empowerment needs to take place. When we empower people, our legacy has a ripple effect of influence that can impact multitudes of people.

I was recently discussing this principle of empowering people for a kingdom ripple effect of influence with three of the young men who were part of my leadership development group. Vuyo, Steve and MK are all former gang members with criminal records – but are now radically transformed and serving God, having all worked with us at The Message. As we discussed the importance of empowering people, they all animatedly spoke of a recent event where they had seen this in action. Vuyo has his own radio show on Radio Tygerberg (a Christian station in Cape Town) and had been asked to organise a community-based outreach in Cape Town's largest township. He took on the challenge and called it an Urban Heroes event... and included a number of ex-gang members in the planning process. The Message was a partner in the event, but the event was entirely organised by those who had once been beneficiaries of our in-prison programme. I attended the event with my family – and was so encouraged to see a packed hall with community members excited to hear the testimonies of our Urban Heroes. But the most impactful part of the afternoon was when Vuyo called forward his organising team – eight young men who all had criminal records. Together they knelt at the front and asked forgiveness from the community for their crimes and on behalf of the terrible acts of violence perpetrated by gang members across Cape Town. As they spoke, mothers began to weep. The audience were visibly impacted. God was at work and perceptions were changed. 'That's the ripple effect of empowering people,' Vuyo told our leadership development meeting. I agree!

Empowering people is not an optional extra for leaders. One company executive who reviewed this book helpfully stated: 'In our company we strive to develop an ethos whereby managers feel that if they were to leave the organisation, the running of their unit would at worst not undergo significant change, and at best, grow to the next level.'[60] An egocentric manager who derives pleasure from things collapsing after he leaves is the antithesis of this ethos. If you have empowered your team members properly, they will grow into greater responsibility once you have 'left the building'! Mature leaders can understand and practise this.

THE JOHN THE BAPTIST PRINCIPLE

One of the greatest examples we have in scripture that illustrate the heart of an empowering leader is that of John the Baptist. John's sole purpose was to prepare the way for Jesus. He was Jesus' cousin who leaped in the womb when he heard Aunt Mary's voice. As he matured, he must have understood from scripture and from divine revelation, that he had a unique mission. It was a mission that would one day involve him stepping away from the limelight in order to allow Jesus, the Messiah, to shine. John had a significant role to play but it would come with much self-sacrifice... ultimately it would cost him his life.

At a critical time in his life, John faced the ultimate test as a leader. He had a fruitful ministry, was gaining a reputation as a prophet and preacher of renown. He had his own disciples, and crowds were coming out to the desert to hear him and be baptised by him. At one point, John's ministry coincided with the onset of Jesus' public ministry, when Jesus began to gain a following. John's disciples were jealous on his behalf and felt threatened by the popularity of Jesus. John had already repeatedly stated that he was not the Messiah, and had even identified Jesus as the One to come, having also testified as such when he baptised Jesus (see John

1:29-34 and Matt. 3:13-17). Now, with his disciples drawing the comparisons and tempting John to stake his own claim as the most popular preacher in Judea, John demonstrates the true self-sacrificial nature of empowering leadership:

> John replied, 'A person can receive only what is given them from heaven. You yourselves testify that I said, 'I am not the Messiah but am sent ahead of him.' The bride belongs to the bridegroom. The friend who attends the bridegroom waits and listens for him, and is full of joy when he hears the bridegroom's voice. That joy is mine, and is now complete. He must become greater; I must become less' (John 3:27-30).

In this statement, John the Baptist demonstrates his calibre as a Christ-centred servant leader. He demonstrated Christ-like character, had a clear sense of his own calling and vision, and was a faithful steward of what had been entrusted to him. With this as his foundation, he was able to demonstrate the heart of someone who empowers others: he was willing to step out of the limelight in order to let Jesus shine – he was genuinely willing to decrease in influence, fame and renown in order for Jesus to flourish. His statement, 'he must become greater, I must become less,' is the principle that all Christ-centred servant leaders need to adopt if they are truly to empower others. This doesn't just happen by chance, it is a conscious decision that leaders need to make if they are genuinely going to raise up other leaders and not just a multitude of followers.

As with everything we've discussed about becoming a Christ-centred servant leader, John's example is completely counter-cultural when compared to contemporary leadership models. Many view leadership as the exercise of power. In contrast, Christ-centred servant leaders follow the John the Baptist principle – they seek to give power away to those that have been raised up and equipped to continue the generational succession planning that is required for the continued expansion of the kingdom, as Jesus intended.

We may think that it was easy for John the Baptist to do this, given that Jesus was his cousin, and more importantly, the Messiah! But what's incredible is that Jesus himself followed the John the Baptist principle. He said to his disciples in John 14:12, 'Very truly I tell you, whoever believes in me will do the works I have been doing, and they will do even greater things than these, because I am going to the Father.' This is surely one of the most jaw-dropping statements in the Bible. How can we possibly do greater things than Jesus? Jesus gave the answer himself by promising to send 'another advocate', the Holy Spirit, who 'lives with you and will be in you' (John 14:16-17).

The Holy Spirit is the ultimate gift of empowerment – a game-changer in history. It was through the empowering of Holy Spirit that the disciples went from being defeated, depressed and disillusioned on the night of Christ's death, to becoming the catalyst for a world-changing movement. As they were baptised in the Holy Spirit at Pentecost, they were empowered and emboldened to proclaim the gospel and challenge people to repent and believe in Jesus Christ. Thousands responded – early evidence of the 'greater things' that Jesus had promised they would do. Kent Hunter emphatically states, 'Jesus is the ultimate leader. The ultimate leader is willing to develop and empower others to the point where they eventually surpass him.'[61]

GIVING POWER AWAY

Empowering others is not an optional extra for Christ-centred servant leaders. Empowering involves giving power away – in the form of position, resources or authority.

Through working with young people in the UK and South Africa, I've learned that to genuinely empower those who have a background in gangs and crime means that we need to provide them with holistic support. This includes sharing the gospel and providing Christian discipleship. Empowerment also means addressing the challenges they face to lead a Christ-centred productive life. So empowerment is a deep process that journeys with someone long-term, seeking to remove all the barriers that could prevent someone from flourishing, and to provide them with a foundation to succeed. As we do this, we begin to see a ripple effect of influence as empowered people are able to in turn impact and empower others. Being faithful stewards means that we will have a multi-generational perspective to our leadership. In following the example of the Apostle Paul (see 2 Tim. 2:2) we should be looking ahead to future generations of leaders. Furthermore, if we want to have a kingdom ripple effect through multiple generations, we need to be committed to being servant leaders who empower our followers to fulfil their potential and even surpass us in their leadership capacity.

What does it take to genuinely empower others? What does this look like practically? It begins with listening to people.

So often, leaders view empowerment as simply allocating projects or tasks to someone who they think they will excel in them. Typically, a leader thinks they know what someone wants to do and then asks them to do it. This is not empowerment – it is simply delegation. Although an important function of leadership, delegation doesn't automatically empower people to fulfil their potential. Leaders can err in making assumptions, and their followers are often too intimidated to speak out and share things about which they are most passionate.

Empowerment always begins with listening. We saw in the previous chapter that listening is a vital component of building trust. Similarly, it is an essential ingredient of empowerment. This is not simply listening to people, hearing their complaints, and then carrying on with business as usual. It is attentive, active and intentional.

Attentive listening means being willing to take time out from your busy schedule and spend time with an individual in order to hear their heart, understand their passion, and engage deeply with them. Attentive listening includes listening to what someone is saying in meetings, presentations and informal conversations.

EMPOWERING OTHERS IS NOT AN OPTIONAL EXTRA FOR CHRIST-CENTRED SERVANT LEADERS

Active listening means engaging with people on subjects that are of interest to them. It involves asking good questions and not always seeking to interrupt with your own opinion. It means delving more deeply, being willing to debate issues or matters, and recognising that we, as leaders, can learn from the other person's perspective.

Intentional listening means that, as you engage with someone, you are also considering how to respond to the information you are receiving. It means prayerfully reflecting on what someone has shared with you with the intention of considering how you can further develop and empower them to fulfil their potential.

As servant leaders listen, they will then be able to encourage people to find solutions for themselves. Leaders need to learn to resist feeling threatened by people who have opinions which are different from their own. It is a mistake to think that they need to have all the best ideas and solutions, and seek to persuade other people that they are the most effective solution-finders in the organisation. This disempowers people and limits the scope of potential solutions.

Few things are more demotivating than expressing an idea to your leader, only for them to summarily dismiss it without considering its merit. Leaders should be open to hearing the words 'I disagree.' They should actively encourage their followers to think critically and not simply accept everything that the leader says without engaging their minds.

Another threat to empowering people is paternalism – when a leader acts like a parent and micro-manages in such a way that it smothers a team's potential. Paternalism is when leaders do things for other people that they are capable of doing for themselves. Paternalism destroys independent thinking. Simply put, Christ-centred servant leaders should 'not do things for people that they can do for themselves.'

The heart of an empowering leader does not worry about who gets the credit, and will celebrate with someone whose ideas succeed – particularly if their way of doing it was different from how the leader would have approached it. True empowerment comes when a team member actualises their potential and is able to say, 'I did it myself!'[62]

As servant leaders listen and provide a platform for people to express their ideas, this should be backed by providing opportunities for people to grow and learn. In Chapter 4 we saw the importance of life-long learning and the role it plays in becoming a deep well of resource as a Christ-centred servant leader. Modelling life-long learning is a way to serve people because it inspires and empowers them to continually invest in their own self-development. Godly leaders will encourage this in their team members.

I've been inspired by my own uncle in this way. In 1998 I moved to South Africa and served as youth pastor in his church. At that time, he was in his 50s and was studying towards a Masters in theology. Once he'd graduated, he then had the opportunity to go on to study his PhD – which he accomplished. Having observed this, it's not surprising that I took his advice when he encouraged me in my own studies. This culminated in 2013 when, at a transitional point in my life, he drove up from Bloemfontein to Pretoria to see me and share that he felt God had given me an opportunity to now pursue my own PhD. Clearly, having witnessed his example, I considered his advice seriously. Within four years I was graduating with my own doctorate in theology. His example empowered me to have the faith that I could also continue to grow and learn, increasing my own capacity as a leader. I trust that my example will empower and inspire others – that's what it means to be Christ-centred servant leader who empowers others to invest in their own development.

LONG-TERM MENTORING[63]

There is no short-term quick-fix way to empower people. Genuine empowerment is a commitment to walk a long road with people – the road of mentoring through providing ongoing support, encouragement and inspiration.

Mentoring is about going deep. It's about deep-well leaders seeking to raise up other deep-well leaders – empowering them to fulfil their potential. But, going deep takes time. It is a road of discipleship. Mentoring involves a substantial investment of time into a small number of people – recognising that this can lead to a ripple effect of influence in the long-term. This follows the example of Jesus, whose 'ultimate mission as a leader was not to develop followers, but to multiply leaders... Jesus modelled going deep with a few, over a long period of time.'[64] Given the level of investment required to raise up effective leaders, it is important that leaders have a well-thought-through process of how they identify those that they will mentor.

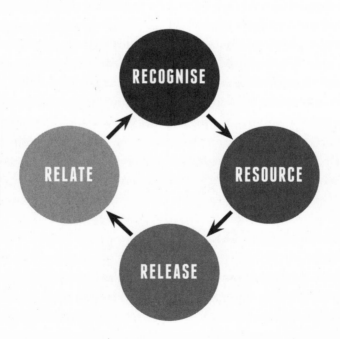

ENSURING FERTILE SOIL

How do we know we are investing in the right people? The task of empowering people can transition through four phases as we mentor emerging leaders – and they all, helpfully, begin with the letter R![65]

RECOGNISE

The first step to effective mentoring is to recognise suitable candidates that can be empowered through your mentorship. At The Message, we call this developing a leadership pipeline and have various methods that we seek to identify potential future leaders. Using the material in this book (which is run as an internal course in various forms at our different branches) is one key way of identifying leaders. We need to expose people to what Christ-centred servant leadership means. Critically, you can't mentor someone who doesn't aspire to grow in their leadership capacity, so facilitating courses and investing in staff development is important in order to stretch people's horizons. However, courses and programmes, as good as they might be, are not sufficient. Once we've recognised those we want to empower, then we invite them into a mentoring process to equip them as leaders.

It's important to consider the criteria that will help you identify emerging leaders as suitable candidates for you to mentor. An obvious starting point is to assess a person's character and to consider how they perform against criteria such as those I presented back in Chapter 1. To what extent are they displaying contentment, humility, accountability, reliability, approachability, consistency, trustworthiness, exemplary conduct and respect? And are they willing to grow in these areas – particularly in the areas in which they are struggling?

It's really important to consider the kind of leaders you want on your team. There are two qualities that I always look for in potential leaders: the ability to take the initiative and teachability. I would rather have someone working with me who is willing to take risks and perhaps make mistakes, than waiting to be told what to do all the time. As Brian Biro says, 'When you use your initiative, you set off a chain reaction in others that leads to true synergy... When you exercise initiative you demonstrate the courage to make decisions and take action, regardless of the odds or the immensity of the challenge before you.'[66]

Teachability may at first seem contradictory to that, but I believe it's entirely complementary. I like people who take the risks that lead to mistakes, but then are humble enough to learn from those mistakes and seek to continually improve. The person who can take initiative but is not teachable is in danger of arrogance, and the person who is teachable but doesn't take initiative is in danger of dependency. The balance between the two affords a sweet spot of opportunity for growth, as the simple continuum below expresses.

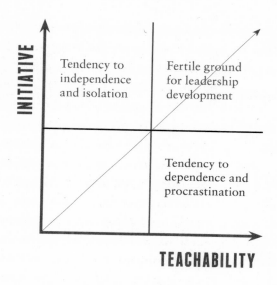

The most important aspect when considering who to mentor, though, is prayer. Sometimes, led by the Holy Spirit, there may be someone you would never have recognised as a potential leader without God's prompting. This was Samuel's experience when God called him to anoint the next king of Israel. All of Jesse's sons seemed more suitable, yet it was David whom God had chosen and who ultimately became the greatest king in Israel's history. As God revealed to Samuel, people look at outward appearances, but God looks at the heart (1 Sam. 16:7).

RESOURCE

To empower emerging leaders, we need to provide them with resources that will enable them to grow, and these resources need to be relevant to their development path.

I recall a Skype session I once had with one of my own mentors. About halfway through the session he emailed me a document. He said that he'd been praying for me that very morning and felt that this document would be good for us to work through together and discuss. You can imagine how encouraged I was – both that he'd been in prayer for me and was seeking to effectively resource me for my own leadership development. I had a similar experience with some executive coaching I received a few years ago. The lady who was mentoring me for that period was constantly seeking to send me relevant and appropriate documents. I also appreciated one leader who I worked under who would always send me books that he thought I would find useful.

ONE OF THE GREATEST RESOURCES WE CAN OFFER A BUDDING LEADER IS TO EMPOWER THEM TO BUILD RELATIONSHIPS WITH OTHER LEADERS

A good mentor will constantly be considering how they can invest in their protégé to help them become a better leader. These resources could be materials, books, introductions to networks or other people, ideas or finance. One of the greatest resources we can offer a budding leader is to empower them to build relationships with other leaders. I have come to understand that the greatest resources I have, outside of God himself, are relationships with people and partners who have joined hands with us on this adventure that God has called us to. Valuing and nurturing the relationships I've formed with friends, supporters, partners and stakeholders is a key leadership task that occupies a large portion of my day. Exposing emerging leaders to these relationships is an invaluable resource that will empower them to reach beyond their horizons. Resources will then flow from these relationships.

Don't forget to help your emerging leader recognise the resources they already have available to them. Many people are sadly debilitated and disempowered because they don't recognise the resources at their disposal. It is easy to think that our job as a mentor is to give, give and give. But this can lead to the dangers of paternalism and dependency. To truly empower someone means that we can help them open their minds to consider how they can best empower themselves. Obviously the greatest resource is your time, so you should never skimp on this if you want to be an effective mentor.

RELEASE

The third key is to release mentees into positions of leadership that will challenge and stretch them. If we consider scripture, we see how Jesus released his disciples when he sent out the Twelve on mission trips, and when he shared in their joy when they realised how God could use them. Likewise, the Apostle Paul, who always had a team of younger emerging leaders such as Timothy and Titus with him, did not hold back his mentees from opportunities to serve, as he knew it would stretch their faith and multiply his effectiveness. As we release people to perform tasks that may at first appear daunting to them, we are helping them to exercise their faith muscles and learn important lessons from both successes and failures.

Releasing people doesn't mean abandoning them. The job of the Christ-centred servant leader is to provide love and support, and be prepared to praise and correct as may be required.

RELATE

The final key is to maintain relationship. Mentorship is about the long haul. However, the nature of the relationship will and should change over time. This is seen with Paul and Barnabas during the golden period of their partnership. Initially we see that Barnabas was the more senior person in the relationship and they were known as Barnabas and Paul (Acts 13:2). However, as the Holy Spirit and Barnabas released Paul into more prominent ministry, the nature of their relationship changed and Luke started to refer to them as Paul and Barnabas. In an ideal situation, even if the mentee becomes more prominent than their mentor, it should not negatively impact a healthy relationship.

I was recently encouraged by a card I received from someone who was part of a youth group I led in Mottram, Manchester, in the mid-90s. As a teenager, Simon was grappling with many of the issues that teens face – but I recognised him as a young man who wanted to faithfully follow God. I don't think I did a particularly amazing job of mentoring him – but I was a listening ear at an important time of his life. Over the years we have kept in touch (social media certainly gives us no excuse for not continuing to relate to people). I was extremely encouraged as Simon established himself, got married, and began a successful career in the non-profit world, working with organisations dealing with important issues like human trafficking. A few years ago we collaborated on a project – no longer as 'youth pastor' and 'young person'... but as equals seeking to serve God in the kingdom. Simon is now based in Canada and does important work with UNICEF – having a kingdom ripple effect. He had read my previous book, and his card simply said, '*Thank you for the book you wrote, which I found helpful, and for being there for me back in the Mottram days of old.'* Not only has continuing to relate to Simon meant we can be co-workers in the gospel (albeit on opposite sides of the globe), but I get the encouragement of knowing that the process of *Recognise, Resource, Release* and *Relate* has had an exponential kingdom ripple effect.

A MATTER OF THE HEART

This process of *Recognise, Resource, Release* and *Relate* provides the opportunity for the leadership development cycle to continue and for the succession of leaders to perpetuate the legacy of Christ and the gospel to the world.

Empowering others is a matter of the heart. It starts with having a deep and genuine desire to have other people surpass us in their effectiveness in the kingdom. This leads us to grab a towel and serve others through finding the most effective ways to empower them which includes listening, encouraging independent thinking, facilitating people to invest in their own development, and providing loving and supportive long-term mentorship. As we give power away, so others will exceed our expectations and even surpass us in their effectiveness and fruitfulness.

CHAPTER 7

LEAD WITH COMPASSION

CHRIST-CENTRED SERVANT LEADERS ARE MOTIVATED BY COMPASSIONATE LOVE FOR OTHERS

'*What matters is the individual. If we wait till we get numbers, then we will be lost in the numbers and we will never be able to show that love and respect for the person*' – *Mother Teresa*[67]

'*He answered, "The one who showed compassion and mercy to him."*' – *Luke 10:36-37 (AMP)*

It might seem rather obvious that we cannot be Christ-centred servant leaders if we do not have compassion. It was compassionate love that caused Jesus to first grab a towel and kneel at the feet of his disciples. It could be argued that compassion was the defining hallmark of Jesus' leadership. But compassion is not often spoken of in leadership books. It can appear too ethereal and intangible, in a world that presents love primarily in romantic terms. Compassion is often associated with sentimentality, and even weakness. Where leaders are expected to be like superheroes or army commandos, there is little room for emotions that are perceived to compromise their authority. But for me, this stems from a misunderstanding of what compassion really is, and overlooks it as an essential and powerful motivational force.

I have been in leadership roles in South Africa for almost twenty years now. In that time, I've hosted numerous international mission teams from western countries and travelled with them to some of the poorest parts of the continent, including Mozambique, Mali and Sudan. Where I now live, in Cape Town, visitors are faced with the challenge of the vast socio-economic divide between the wealthy and the poor. This can cause strong emotional responses from visitors – ranging from sympathy to anger to guilt. Many would describe feeling compassion for those who are less fortunate than themselves. But my personal experience has shown me that, when you live in a particular context for a long period of time, it is easy for the things that once caused an emotional response to simply become the norm. We can become desensitised to the injustices and unfairness of life. The emotional response is no longer stimulated because we become familiar with the surroundings in which we live. Does this mean that we can no longer be compassionate? I don't think so.

What I explain to the visiting teams is that compassion is not merely based on feelings. Rather, compassion is a decision that is sometimes stirred by feelings, but often is an intentional choice. I must choose every day to not become immune to the challenges of poverty and the scale of injustice in the city in which I live. Compassion is a decision to seek to respond to the situation in a loving way.

For example, The Message seeks to impact the least, last and lost because, a) we have been moved by the fact that urban teenagers are heading towards a Christ-less eternity, b) we believe that God has called us to act, and c) we have a strategy to use our gifts and talents in ways that will make a practical difference in the lives of tens of thousands of young people. I would argue that these three components are all critical in being an organisation characterised by compassion. If we relied just on one component, then we would not be able to sustain a loving response to the challenges we see in the world.

I always encourage visiting teams and volunteers with the view that the only way to truly be compassionate is to make the decision to follow the advice of Paul: 'Therefore, as God's chosen people, holy and dearly loved, clothe yourselves with compassion, kindness, humility, gentleness and patience' (Col. 3:12). We are to take the decision every day to figuratively clothe ourselves with compassion. This shows that compassion is not an intrinsic (or internal) response to our emotions, but an extrinsic (or external)

decision that we make. Just as we wouldn't leave our homes in the morning without getting dressed in physical clothes, so we are not ready to face the world as a Christ-centred servant leader unless we have clothed ourselves with compassion. This is even more critical for leaders who have walked the long road of leadership that is lined with disappointments, tough breaks, failure and exhaustion. The only way to maintain a passionate heart when faced with the daily realities of leadership is continually to make a choice to be a compassionate leader.

THE ONLY WAY TO MAINTAIN A PASSIONATE HEART IS CONTINUALLY TO MAKE A CHOICE TO BE A COMPASSIONATE LEADER

With a transformed heart and clothed with compassion, we are equipped to grab a towel as we engage the world and become Christ-centred servant leaders. 'Compassionate love is the axis of the Christian moral revolution and the only sign ever given by Jesus by which a disciple would be recognised.'[68] Simply put, the motivation for Christ-centred servant leaders is compassion.

THE FUEL OF CHRIST-CENTRED LEADERSHIP

The Bible teaches us that God is full of compassion – it is one of his defining characteristics in the Old Testament. God reveals himself to Moses as 'the LORD, the compassionate and gracious God...' (Ex. 34:6). Psalm 145:8 likewise says, 'The LORD is good to all; he has compassion on all he has made'. Paul describes God as the 'Father of compassion' (2 Cor. 1:3). God loves us and his compassion is expressed through his gracious intervention in the world and in our lives.

In the gospels, we see Jesus modelling the compassion of God. Matthew 9:36-39 says:

> When he saw the crowds, he had compassion on them, because they were harassed and helpless, like sheep without a shepherd. Then he said to his disciples, 'The harvest is plentiful but the workers are few. Ask the Lord of the harvest, therefore, to send out workers into his harvest field.'

Here we see one practical response that all Christ-centred servant leaders need to do to fuel and express their compassion: pray! Our prayers are effective if they are fuelled by loving compassion. And we can sustain a compassionate response through prayer because we are connecting to God's heart – God who is the Father of compassion. Compassionate leaders are praying leaders; similarly, praying leaders are compassionate leaders. This is a challenge for all of us. Are we praying for our teams (and not just that they'll become better employees)? Are we praying for our organisation? Are we praying for the church in our area? Are we praying for the communities we work in, the countries, other leaders and organisations?

Jesus was not only stirred by compassion, but he also acted in response to the compassion he felt. For example, in Matthew 14:14 we read, 'When Jesus landed and saw a large crowd, he had compassion on them and healed their sick.' *Compassionate action is the evidence of a loving heart.* Jesus' compassion led him to action. Ultimately, it was his compassion for us that took him to the cross – the ultimate act of compassionate love. Through that one loving act, he has transformed the destiny of the human race. Therefore, compassion is not merely a feeling of sympathy but motivates leaders to change the circumstances of those in need. It moves us beyond simply trying to appease our conscience with thoughtless acts of charity. As Martin Luther King famously stated, 'True compassion is more than flinging a coin to a beggar; it is not haphazard and... it comes to see that an edifice which produces beggars needs restructuring.'[69] In other words, having the compassion of Christ will change the way we view the world and motivates us to fulfil God's calling to be his ambassadors in the world (2 Cor. 5:17-20).

In order to become compassionate leaders we ourselves need to be the recipients of the compassion of Christ. According to Ezekiel 36:26, this involves having a heart transplant! We need to pray that God will transform our hard hearts into hearts of flesh.

TO WHOM DO WE SHOW COMPASSION?

In Luke 10:25-37, Jesus gives us one of his most famous parables – the parable of the Good Samaritan. It is a parable that stands the test of time as a challenging illustration of godly self-sacrificial love. The parable is a preacher's dream as one can draw out numerous points relating to how godly love stands in contrast to the social and religious stigma that brings division to the human race (and is sadly often demonstrated in the church). The Good Samaritan himself is an anonymous hero who shows unconditional love to someone he should have despised. Not only does he tend to the immediate needs of the injured man, but he goes above and beyond what is required, ensuring that the man who should have been his enemy convalesces to full recovery.

The story is powerful, yet it needs to be held within the context of the discussion that Jesus had with an 'expert in the law' who was seeking to 'test Jesus'. Here was a Jewish leader – probably a good man by most people's standards – who undoubtedly had passionate religious zeal. He loved the Word of God and sought to follow it to the letter. His question, 'What must I do to inherit eternal life?' demanded a response from Jesus. It was a question deliberately formed to test the credentials of this upstart rabbi from Nazareth who was causing such a stir in Judea and beginning to gain a significant following. Yet the question also betrays the man's heart: formed in a self-centred manner, he was chiefly concerned with his own status rather than having a heart for others.

So we see that this scriptural narrative is not simply a contrast between the Good Samaritan and the other characters in the story (the priest and the Levite), but it demonstrates the contrast between Jesus' approach to leadership and the approach of the Jewish leaders of the day.

Here is the narrative between Jesus and the expert in the law (editing out the parable itself):

> And a certain lawyer [an expert in Mosaic Law] stood up to test Him, saying, 'Teacher, what must I do to inherit eternal life?'
> Jesus said to him, 'What is written in the Law? How do you read it?'
> And he replied, 'You shall love the Lord your God with all your heart, and with all your soul, and with all your

strength, and with all your mind; and your neighbour as
yourself.'

Jesus said to him, 'You have answered correctly; do this
habitually and you will live.' But he, wishing to justify
and vindicate himself, asked Jesus, 'And who is my
neighbour?'

[following the parable, Jesus asked him] 'Which of these
three do you think proved himself a neighbour to the
man who encountered the robbers?'

He answered, 'The one who showed compassion and
mercy to him.'

Then Jesus said to him, 'Go and constantly do the
same.'[70]

The story identifies the essence of their different approaches to life
and leadership; the 'expert in the law' had a limited understanding
of who his neighbour was. He defined this through a homogenous
cultural lens – he loved those who were like him and sought to
lead and influence those who behaved and looked like him. Jesus
exploded this myth. He demonstrates that kingdom leadership is
demonstrated through having a broad and heterogeneous understanding of what it means to love one's neighbour.

The motivation for Christ-centred servant leadership is, therefore, love of God expressed through practical love for other people
(our neighbours), which should especially include those who are
different, downcast and desolate.

The contrast between the expert in the law and Jesus is particularly relevant in our fragmented and compartmentalised world.
We need leaders who will become bridge-builders and cross the
barriers that divide people by cultural, economic and other means.

As Paul said, we are 'compelled by the love of Christ' because we have an inclusive understanding of the gospel that it is available to everyone (see 2 Cor. 5:14). In particular, our Christian leaders need to take note of the Bible's consistent commands to show neighbourly love to the poor and marginalised.

This is particularly relevant for those of us who live and lead in Africa. In recent times there has been so much negativity towards the continent of Africa. Following centuries of destructive colonial influence and interference, there are undoubtedly huge challenges facing the people of this continent. The scale of poverty, the spread of disease and the scourge of corruption continues to plague many countries. There has been an enormous amount of financial aid given over the past 50 years which does not seem to have improved the problems but rather seems to have exacerbated them. However, in my experience, many Africans are incredibly tenacious, hardworking and fully committed to seeing this continent rise. There is massive leadership potential, particularly among young entrepreneurs who are seeking to build a better future in the continent. Rather than being pessimistic about the future of this continent, I believe there is cause for optimism as God is raising up transformational Christ-centred servant leaders who will influence and shape the destiny of this beautiful continent. At The Message we are 'Afri-optimistic' and pray that Christian leaders around the world will seek to genuinely empower African leaders as an act of neighbourly love.

It is one thing to understand that loving our neighbour is a non-negotiable facet of being a Christ-centred servant leader, but applying this practically can be quite a different thing. So we need to ask the questions, how do we express compassion as leaders and how do we foster an environment within our organisations that enables us to genuinely love other people?

COMPASSION LEADING TO KINSHIP

In 2015 I had the privilege to meet one man who exemplifies compassionate leadership. Father Gregory Boyle is the founder of Homeboy Industries in Los Angeles. For over twenty years he has worked with gang members from some of the toughest neighbourhoods in LA. Homeboy Industries provides hope and opportunity for former gang members who want a fresh start (understandably, we at The Message are quite taken with Homeboys!) and provides an environment of love and acceptance. It is Father Boyle's own avuncular and compassionate leadership that draws people into Homeboy to experience the contrast from the life of fear and violence that is the language of the gangs.

> **LEADERS ARE NOT SUPERHEROES WHO FIX PROBLEMS, BUT CHRIST-FOCUSED SERVANTS WHO LEAD PEOPLE TO JESUS**

However, this is no bed-of-roses ministry. Father Boyle has had to bury hundreds of gang members and other innocents caught up in gang warfare over the years. He speaks with gravitas on the subject of compassion because he has faced the destructive forces of evil and continues to seek to overcome it with love. His starting point for compassion is to move away from a judgemental attitude and have a fresh perspective: 'Here is what we seek: a compassion that can stand in awe at what the poor have to carry rather than stand in judgement at how they carry it.'[71]

His ministry philosophy seeks to counter the negative and destructive cycle of gangsterism by providing a Christ-centred alternative: that of kinship. With the practice of kinship he moves beyond merely serving others, to standing with them in their pain and suffering. He draws on the example of Christ as his inspiration for kinship:

> Jesus was not a man for others. He was one with others. There is a world of difference in that. Jesus didn't seek the rights of lepers. He touched the leper even before he got around to curing him. He didn't champion the cause of the outcast. He was the outcast. He didn't fight for improved conditions for the prisoner. He simply said, 'I was in prison'.[72]

The challenge for Christ-centred servant leaders is to move towards people in their pain and suffering. It is not simply about having the right attitude or correct theories. It is about standing in the right position.[73] As in the story of the Good Samaritan, it is about removing the barriers that divide us in order to open ourselves more fully to others.

Yet, on an even deeper level, Christ-centred servant leaders must also recognise their own insecurities, pain and sinfulness. In identifying with the broken, we recognise our own brokenness. Leaders are not superheroes who fix problems, but Christ-focused servants who lead people to Jesus and empower them to grow in their relationship with him. As Father Boyle has demonstrated, kinship moves beyond a one-way relationship between you as the solution-based leader and a so-called beneficiary. Compassion, expressed through kinship, is a covenant between equals.[74]

THE POWER OF ONE

You might be reading this and still find yourself overwhelmed. Yes – you want to be a compassionate leader that is fuelled with love like Father Gregory Boyle, or even Jesus! But the challenge appears overwhelming. Where do we start? Perhaps you've also had negative experiences along the way – maybe you feel a bit like Linus in the Charlie Brown comic strip who said: 'I do love mankind – it's people I can't stand!' The reality is that compassionate leadership is best expressed in love for individuals. When people become overwhelmed by the scale of injustice, poverty, crime, disease and suffering in the world, we should recall the simple words of Joel Manby who says, 'Do for one what you wish you could do for everyone.'[75]

As we've entered the 21st century and continue to face the massive challenges of poverty and inequality in the world, much has been written about 'Making Poverty History'. Ash Barker, who spent many years living in a slum in Thailand and now lives on a tough housing estate in England, has said that we need to make poverty personal before we can make it history. As I have been leading Message South Africa, amidst the huge challenges of inequality that exist in the aftermath of apartheid, I have become convinced that what this country needs is a redistribution of relationships as well as a redistribution of resources. Relationships are fundamental to showing genuine love.

As we have seen, the story of the Good Samaritan is a sublime example of compassionate love expressed in doing for one person what we wish we could do for everyone. As Christ-centred servant leaders we have a mandate to express compassionate love to individuals. This includes those we are leading in our organisations.

We must not see our teams as homogenous groups of co-workers that we treat in a uniform way. Rather, we should engage people as individuals and ask God for insight into how we can help each person fulfil their potential.

Additionally, as Christ-centred servant leaders we should demonstrate compassionate love to those less fortunate than ourselves. However, just as the compassionate love of Christ has been rejected by billions of people through the centuries, we also need to recognise that we have no guarantees that our acts of kindness and service won't be manipulated, rejected and even abused. We ultimately need to remember that it is Christ we are serving, and this enables us to not get disillusioned and stick it out to lead with love over the long haul, which is the topic of my final chapter.

FROM COMPASSION TO TRANSFORMATION

There is a symbiotic relationship between compassion and relationships. Compassion is often initially aroused because of exposure to the challenges someone faces. But, as we deepen our relationships and seek to stand with people in their challenges and pain, so we will find that our perspectives and assumptions become transformed, enabling us to become more compassionate. I am a little concerned by the conventional wisdom that 'Leadership is a lonely place.' Yes – there are times when leaders need to have the resolve to stand alone in their convictions when all around them think they are crazy. But this should not be the norm when we consider the example of Jesus. For Christ-centred servant leaders, relationships are critical. It was from the foundation of loving relationships amidst diverse cultural backgrounds, that the early church had 'everything in common' and was able to share its possessions: 'they gave to anyone as he had need' (Acts 2:42-45). The loneliness of leadership is a contradiction in terms for Christ-centred servant leaders who are grabbing a towel to express compassionate love to others.

From the foundation of loving relationships, it is then important to reflect deeply on how to genuinely empower people through generous support. Although giving generously to anyone in dire need is not necessarily wrong, simply giving of money in a haphazard way can actually contribute to problems rather than solve them. As I discussed in the previous chapter, empowerment is not doing for people what they can do for themselves. Nor is it putting a Band-Aid on deep gushing wounds.

We again need to remember that Christ-centred servant leaders are not superheroes who are trying to solve every problem. Ash Barker teaches that, as Christians, we are not called to solve every problem, but rather to be a signpost that points people to the One in whom all people can find peace, reconciliation and restitution. However, being a signpost means we have to be visible, involved and engaged in communities that are gripped by poverty and injustice.

In 2014, we launched our first Eden Team in South Africa. An Eden team is a group of urban missionaries who move into a tough neighbourhood in order to present the love of Jesus in action and word.[76] They aim to follow the example of Christ as described by John: 'The Word became flesh and moved into the neighbourhood' (John 1:14, MSG). The community they moved in to is a historically deprived, largely Muslim community, with young people caught up in gang activity and drug addiction. However, it is also a community that is becoming increasingly gentrified due to the close proximity to the city centre. The team came from diverse backgrounds and took about a year to form, move in, and settle in the community. As The Message, we did not tell the team what to do or give them specific programmes through which to bring transformation. Rather, they entered the communities as neighbours. They built relationships. They listened to people and to God. They prayer walked, had conversations, offered hospitality and connected with young people. They committed long-term and have therefore found relevant ways to share the gospel.[77] As relationships have been formed, this has led the team to engage in various activities – serving the community through joining the local football team and coaching kids, offering educational support to local schools, starting a dance group and various ongoing relational connections with young people. The most recent developments have included launching a coffee shop and seeking to address the challenge of gentrification by seeking to provide affordable housing. I look on amazed at what God is doing through this team of compassionate Christ-centred leaders who didn't claim to have solutions, but were prepared to be signposts of God's grace and love within a broken community.

COMPASSION – ESSENTIAL FOR THE LONG HAUL

Leading with compassion is critical in order to be a Christ-like servant leader who is seeking to grow in all the ways that we've presented in this book. A Christian leader with a compassionate heart has a mandate to show love to those from poor and difficult backgrounds. Community transformation does not occur by a 'macro' plan imposed by superhero leaders. Rather, it occurs as we engage deeply with people and commit to serving them over the long haul. Success is not guaranteed, but we can be signposts, pointing people to Jesus Christ who personified and defined self-sacrificial love.[78]

William Booth, the founder of the Salvation Army, was an incredible man of faith who tirelessly preached the gospel and developed practical opportunities to improve the lives of the poorest of the poor. Yet what was his motivation? The heart behind the man is expressed in this often-quoted excerpt of a message he gave – reputed to be from his final sermon:

> 'While women weep, as they do now, I'll fight. While little children go hungry, as they do now, I'll fight. While men go to prison, in and out, in and out, as they do now, I'll fight. While there is a drunkard left, while there is a poor lost girl upon the streets, while there remains one dark soul without the light of God, I'll fight – I'll fight to the very end!'[79]

His compassionate heart for abused women, hungry children, imprisoned men, alcoholic homeless people, and the countless number of people facing a Christless eternity, expresses the underlying motivation that he had: his vertical love for God which was then expressed in horizontal, practical love for his neighbour.

Having a compassionate heart is essential if we want to maintain our motivation as Christ-centred servant leaders who can stick it out through the turbulent waters we have to navigate as leaders.

CHAPTER 8

HAVE STEEL IN YOUR SPINE

CHRIST-CENTRED SERVANT LEADERS HAVE THE STEELY RESOLVE TO PERSEVERE

'I can plod.' – William Carey[80]

'But one thing I do: Forgetting what is behind and straining toward what is ahead, I press on toward the goal to win the prize for which God has called me heavenward in Christ Jesus.' –Philippians 3:13–14

Each year at Message South Africa we ask God to give us a theme and key passage of scripture for the year. We explore the theme at our monthly prayer days, which serves as a useful method of fostering team unity. In 2016 our theme was 'Revived to Thrive', based on a story about the Old Testament king, Hezekiah.

Hezekiah was an amazing biblical character. He succeeded the throne from his father, Ahaz, around 720 BC. Ahaz was a disastrous king on every level – spiritually and politically. Judah was severely compromised in their faith and through their alliances with other ungodly nations. The global power at the time was Assyria, and Judah was like putty in their hands. Hezekiah inherited a nation in deep trouble. However, as a young man (just 25 when he became king) he led the nation in wholesale changes... in spiritual, moral and political revival. He restored the temple and worship of the Lord. Over a 14-year period he led from the front, serving the people through an example of godly leadership. When the people rededicated the temple and their lives to God, Hezekiah's influence is recorded for posterity: 'There was great joy in Jerusalem, for since the days of Solomon son of David king of Israel there had been nothing like this in Jerusalem' (2 Chr. 30:26). High praise indeed!

However, Hezekiah's biggest leadership test remained ahead of him. His reforms and the spiritual revival he'd initiated would not go unnoticed by the Assyrian superpower. Pretty soon the might of Sennacherib, king of Assyria, was focused against Jerusalem. In the face of daunting military power and the threat of annihilation, Hezekiah kept the faith. He prayed, applied strategic skill, and communicated confidence to his subjects and fellow citizens. Our key verses for that year were 2 Chronicles 32:7-8 where Hezekiah addresses the people and says:

> 'Be strong and courageous. Do not be afraid of the king of Assyria and the vast army with him, for there is a greater power with us than with him. With him is only the arm of flesh, but with us is the LORD our God to help us and to fight our battles.' And the people gained confidence from what Hezekiah the king of Judah said.

The Message version puts this last sentence beautifully: 'Morale surged. Hezekiah's words put steel in their spines.' (2 Chronicles 32:8, MSG.)

Hezekiah's example of godly leadership ensured his people kept the faith during extremely trying times. This is an integral component of becoming a Christ-centred servant leader. Tough times will come! Will we keep the faith and inspire others to do likewise? Will we set an example that gives people confidence and puts 'steel in their spines' – a rigid resolve to remain faithful to God no matter what? If you are a leader, it is inevitable that there are going to be times when you simply have to stick it out – persevere with steel in your spine. That is what Hezekiah did – and his confidence was vindicated as God answered his prayers and dealt with the enemy in a manner that ensured all the people knew that it was God who had secured the victory.

As we reflected on this passage during the first six months of 2016, we were unaware that, as a team, we would need to fully embrace the example of Hezekiah – and, for me personally, in a particularly traumatic way.

In August 2016, my wife Laura suddenly and unexpectedly passed away. Clearly nothing can prepare you for such a significant life-changing event. Although she had been unwell, there was nothing to indicate that she would die from a brain aneurysm.

IF YOU ARE A LEADER IT IS INEVITABLE THAT THERE ARE GOING TO BE TIMES WHEN YOU SIMPLY HAVE TO STICK IT OUT

We were on a long-anticipated holiday with my brother's family. We were on the beach on Tuesday, in hospital all day Wednesday, and Laura passed away early on Thursday morning.

The event was not only traumatic for me, our children and the immediate family, but also for the broader community of our church, The Message and our friends around the world. A young mother suddenly losing her life brings home everyone's sense of mortality and causes us to ask deep questions. For me personally, it was not a test of my faith so much as the beginning of a journey to more deeply understand God's perspective on death, life, suffering, joy, peace, pain and hope – and learning how God was my ally throughout this most painful of times. Yes, I had the assurance that Laura was at peace in Christ's presence, but I had to face the reality of a new life – one that I hadn't chosen and that I was unprepared for.

There were a few specific moments where I recall the importance of having 'steel in my spine', the resolve to keep the faith and stick it out no matter what. The first was at the memorial service when I stood in front of the gathered community, with my children by my side, to pay tribute to my incredible late wife. I wanted to be honest, yet faithful to God, recognising that the words I chose would carry weight as a testimony to where our true hope lay through such a difficult time. It was a leadership moment where, in my weakness, I asked God to strengthen me in order to be faithful to him. I felt God strengthened us as a family and it was incredibly bonding to state in public that we would survive, we would not give up and that, in spite of not having all the answers, we would continue to trust in God.

A few months later we spent Christmas in England with family. It was a transition time, preparing to return to South Africa and face an uncertain future as we sought to discover what our new life would hold. People often say that you face the *'new normal'* after the loss of a loved one – I rather call it the *'new abnormal.'* I remember boarding the plane to return to South Africa and having to dig deep to find the resolve that we would face this future, a future we hadn't chosen. It was a tough period with lots of change (new schools for the children and a new life as a single dad for me) and I needed steel in my spine to lead my family at this time.

More recently, having returned to work and resumed leadership of Message South Africa, we were preparing for our annual Vision Night event. This is where we showcase and celebrate all that God is doing through The Message. Since the memorial, I had stepped back from public speaking and direct leadership of the organisation. Now, six months later, I was to give the keynote address, share the vision, and ask people to support us in prayer and finances. My emotions were made more complex because the venue was the church where the memorial had been held, so I'd be speaking from the very stage where I'd stood with the children just a few months earlier. It was tough. I remember, before the event, going into the prayer room where we had our Message intercessors seeking God on behalf of the event. I felt vulnerable and weak but, as they prayed for me, I felt the steel return to my spine and the confidence surface again that, as leader of the mission, God would give me strength through my weakness to inspire confidence and faith that God is able to lift us from the ashes and enable us to fulfil the work he had called us to do.

Who knew that our year of 'Revived to Thrive' would lead us through such troubled waters? As I reflect on 2016 I still can't give simple answers as to why God allowed such a deep test of my faith – one which will continue to bring me and my family painful moments, even amidst the joy and hope that we all have for the future. Nevertheless, I see the fruit of knowing that God walked with us through the trial – not just for me, but also for the Message

SA team. While I was side-lined, the team had to step up – and they did thrive even in a time of great adversity. Also, it wasn't just me who suffered through difficult circumstances. A number of our team also went through deeply difficult experiences that year and it was incredible to see how their faith was refined and how, as a team, we experienced the deep love and grace of God amidst deep times of difficulty. We emerged more determined than ever to serve God with steel in our spines to confidently profess his grace and goodness to our generation. We have a resilience because we've faced the onslaught of the evil one and, although we have the scars, we are still standing thanks to God's grace. We have renewed determination that comes from having 'steel in our spine' and that we'll continue to serve God and see the gospel impact young people across Cape Town and beyond.

I have shared my experience quite extensively because this is where the rubber of leadership theory hits the road of the reality of life. I sincerely believe that becoming a Christ-centred servant leader is the only way to have 'steel in our spine' to continue through both the tragedies and triumphs of life. As Hezekiah demonstrated, the confident faith of the people was directly proportional to him directing them to trust God. His ultimate act of service was to not try and answer all their questions or calm their fears, but to direct them to put their trust and hope in God. Through that act of service, the people's confidence surged and they had steel in their spines.

In times of the greatest difficulty, leaders must keep their focus on Christ as that is the ultimate way to serve people. We serve people by continually turning their gaze towards Jesus. As our leader, he himself had the wisdom and love to warn us with an imperative promise, 'Here on earth you will have many trials and sorrows', but then give us the courage and key to having steel in our spines by assuring us in saying, 'But take heart because I have overcome the world' (John 16:33).

Being a strong leader doesn't mean we have all the answers, but that, in our weakness and disappointments, we can still point people to our ultimate leader in whom we find peace and hope.

GRITTY LEADERSHIP

Bill Hybels calls this being a 'gritty leader', and he names it as an essential intangible of leadership. If we are to stick it out – and be leaders that go the distance – we need to have the gritty determination and tenacity to keep going through trying situations. I agree with him when he states that the enemy of grit is ease, and as Christian leaders we are not called to lead people to a life of ease, but rather to a life of peace where we are certain that Jesus is in control, even if our current circumstances seem to contradict that.

Christ-centred servant leaders have a steely determination because they recognise they are in it for the long haul. There are no quick-fix solutions to the challenges we face in the world today. The reality is that God develops our grit through bringing circumstances and situations which develop our character and test our perseverance. If we consider a few biblical examples, we will see that every leader developed steel in their spine as they endured in the school of hard knocks!

- Abraham left his homeland and became nomadic, facing challenges of drought, war and requiring continued patience for the fulfilment of God's promises to him – particularly for the birth of his son.

- Joseph was sold by his brothers into slavery and then imprisoned after a false accusation of rape.
- David's life was under threat from King Saul and he had to live on the run as a refugee in enemy territory.
- Nehemiah was constantly criticised and undermined by his enemies who ultimately sought to take his life.
- Mary had to face the humiliation of being pregnant before marriage and her fiancé preparing to call off the wedding.
- Paul had a massive catalogue of challenges that threatened his life and undermined his ministry. These included natural disasters, persecution, criticism and spiritual discouragement. He said 'I press on' in spite of all these challenges (see Phil. 3:12-14).

Although God is not the author of evil events or disaster, he is ultimately sovereign and able to turn all things around – redeeming the most terrible of situations. It is from this understanding that Paul is able to state that we can 'glory in our sufferings' (Rom. 5:3) because God uses them to develop perseverance, character and hope – in other words, grit and steel in our spines.

SUBMISSION TO GOD IS ESSENTIAL IF WE ARE TO BE GRITTY LEADERS WHO STICK IT OUT FOR THE LONG HAUL

During his ministry, Jesus faced adversity from his family, his disciples, the people, and both religious and political officials seeking to destroy him. Grit was essential in maintaining focus on his mission during those challenging times. There is no better example of gritty leadership. Christ endured the cross and fulfilled his God-given mission to die for humanity, which brought restoration to God through the forgiveness of our sins. Faith and hope combined to bring joy.

We learn from Jesus' example that leaders grow in endurance and perseverance through having the same attitude that he had. Jesus was fully submitted to the Father. We see this on the Mount of Olives when he was facing the agony of the cross. Jesus asked God to remove the burden from him (a normal response when facing overwhelming pain), but still had the faith to say, 'Not my will, but yours be done' (Luke 22:42). Submission to God is essential if we are to be gritty leaders who stick it out for the long haul. Jesus looked beyond the pain and suffering to the prize upon which he was focused – namely, our salvation and restoration to God. Hebrews 12:2 says that Jesus could persevere with steel in his spine because he was keeping his eyes on 'the joy set before him'. The Message translation puts it this way: 'Because he never lost sight of where he was headed – that exhilarating finish in and with God – he could put up with anything along the way: Cross, shame, whatever.' (Hebrews 12:2, MSG.)

When you know where you are headed, you are able to continue with gritty determination and stick it out with steel in your spine.

THE DANGER OF GRIT

There is also a danger of overemphasis on this quality of grit, however. Bill Hybels says, 'Gritty people play hurt, they don't whimper, or waver, or quit... ever.'[81] I tend to disagree with this view. After my wife died, I didn't play hurt. I took time out to focus on God and the priorities that would help me endure. That was my main concern as a Christ-centred servant leader. If I'd have continued to play hurt then I may simply have hurt others and not served people well. I needed time and space – and it took steel in my spine to be honest about that and not try to conjure up some superhuman strength. As I've tried to demonstrate through this book, that is the antithesis of Christ-centred servant leadership.

There are many examples in the Bible of leaders taking the time to recover and restore their strength in God in order to endure and stick it out for the long haul. Perhaps Elijah gives us the greatest example of a man who, after a time of intense public ministry, had to withdraw and allow God to minister to him in his pain, in order that he could be re-envisioned and commissioned to endure (see 1 Kings 19). However, we can clearly grow in our gritty determination to serve God and stick it out. As we submit to God's will and keep focused on the prize ahead, he will lead us through processes which will enable us to be leaders with steel in our spines.

FAITH: LOOKING TO GOD IN THE TOUGH TIMES

Faith is essential if we want to be Christ-centred servant leaders with steel in our spines – in fact, faith and Christ-centred servant leadership are directly proportional to each other. Hebrews 11:1 says that 'faith is confidence in what we hope for and assurance about what we do not see'. Christ-centred servant leaders do not focus on confidence in themselves, but rather continually grow in their confidence and dependence on God, which means they grow in faith. As is often stated, faith is like a muscle that develops the more it is used.

It is possible to adapt a quote of Jim Collins to how faith is developed. He says, 'Greatness is not primarily a matter of circumstances; greatness is first and foremost a matter of conscious choice and discipline'.[82] We can say that 'faith is not primarily a matter of circumstances; faith [in God] is first and foremost a matter of conscious choice and discipline'. In other words, we don't grow in faith if we rely on our feelings... we grow in faith in direct proportion to our choice to continue to trust God and in applying discipline to act in obedience to him even when it seems illogical.

Christ-centred servant leaders need to keep the faith even when it seems like things are crumbling around us, when things don't go to plan, when we're under financial or organisational pressure, or when we are let down by others. It is easy to lead when things are going well but the true test of our faith is when everything seems to be going wrong. Faith requires that we hold on to our convictions and keep acting in a way consistent to our character. Peter states that trials can come in order to 'prove the genuineness of your faith' (1 Pet. 1:7).

In the difficult periods of life and leadership it's important that we take time to strengthen and increase our faith. This begins with prayer – perhaps using the helpful prayer of the father of the possessed child who approached Jesus to heal his son, 'I do believe, help me overcome my unbelief' (Mark 9:24). That's a beautiful prayer for a Christ-centred leader... we are at one and the same time to exert faith and recognise our utter dependence on God. We also strengthen our faith through spending time with God, listening to him, reflecting on our circumstances and committing everything to God, reading the Word and remembering his promises and prophetic words.

Although faith will require action, it is imperative that action does not precede seeking God. We saw earlier how Hezekiah responded to the Assyrian threat – his first instinct was to seek God. This should be the first instinct of all Christ-centred servant leaders and the only sure way that we will be strengthened in our faith and resolve to face every challenge with steel in our spines.

FAILURE: GETTING BACK UP AGAIN

Christ-centred servant leaders recognise that failure *is* an option and that failure can be an important process through which God shapes our character and reliance on him. Leaders with steel in their spine won't let failure define them, but see failure as an opportunity to learn and grow. Thomas Edison famously failed many times before successfully inventing the light bulb... he had steel in his spine. American president Abraham Lincoln lost eight elections, failed in two businesses and suffered a nervous break-down which left him bedridden for six months. But if he'd given up, American history might look very different.

In the Bible we see the glaring failings of many heroes of the faith, from Moses the murderer through to the three denials of Peter. We can identify with the failings of biblical men and women who were regular people just like us. Just like Moses, Jonah, Zechariah (John the Baptist's father), Peter, and hundreds of thousands of Christians through history, we can learn that failure is not terminal and can actually be the springboard for leaders to fulfil their potential.

The danger of this book is that you may think we have presented The Message as an organisation to emulate because we are perfectly implementing Christ-centred servant leadership. But most of the lessons on servant leadership in this book were learned in God's school of hard knocks, and we are still learning (and far from perfect!). Dan Palotta argues that this is not just true for the leaders within an organisation, but that there needs to be a culture that allows failure when team members are innovating in pursuit of the organisation's goals. He says, 'When you prohibit failure you kill innovation.'[83] Helping people learn and grow from failure is one of the best ways we can serve them and enable them to grow and mature in faith and life.

In writing this book I am very conscious that my own journey has included a catalogue of failings where I haven't lived up to the model of Christ-centred servant leadership presented here. I can recall times when I haven't put people first, when I've led in my own strength, and when I haven't empowered or loved people as I should have. And beside a myriad of small failings, there were some huge clangers along the way when I could do nothing but hold my hands up and say, 'Wow, I got that wrong!'

Christ-centred servant leaders will make mistakes. Although aspiring to be like Jesus, we are not Jesus! But, if we recognise that we are not defined by failure but can be propelled to push forward in spite of our failures, then we are in a powerful position to keep growing and learning. As the Blackabys put it:

'Successful leaders are not successful because they never err in judgement, but because they continually learn from their mistakes. Mistakes made once become catalysts for personal growth and future success. The same mistakes, made repeatedly, are inexcusable.'[84]

Great leaders not only confess that they fail, but also repent (where necessary), admit their mistakes to others, and resolve to learn in order that they can move forward with courage and the confidence of their teams.

Being a servant leader with steel in your spine requires seeing failure as part of the leadership process. Failure enables us to learn and become better leaders. Sometimes we need to take risks that might simply not work out, but leaders will bounce back and continue to take calculated risks because we realise that losing one battle does not mean losing the war.

FIGHT: PUSHING THROUGH

I'm not sure if Paul was a boxing fan but he did enjoy using metaphors from wrestling and boxing. In 2 Timothy 4:7, as he was contemplating his impending death at the hands of a Roman executioner, he stated, 'I have fought the good fight, I have finished the race, I have kept the faith.'

Christ-centred servant leaders are engaged in a good fight. It is ultimately a fight for souls, for the eternal destiny of countless millions of people. I believe the principles laid out in this book are worth fighting for. Representing Jesus in this world is worth fighting for. Seeing broken individuals and communities restored through the gospel is worth fighting for. Young people, caught up in gangs, crime, substance abuse and self-harm are worth fighting for. In fact – it's imperative that we fight the good fight! The fight takes place in the spiritual realm through prayer and also in the physical realm through hard work, grit, determined effort and perseverance. The fight also includes demonstrating unconditional love, not giving up on people, and enduring in hope. These things will come to define us as we seek to lead with steel in our spines.

I am glad to be part of an organisation that is committed to fighting the good fight. We will fight for young people who do not know Christ and are caught up in a downward spiral of destructive behaviour. We will fight for them to hear the gospel in language they can understand and to experience love from people who genuinely care for them. We will fight for them to have opportunities to overcome every barrier they face to become contrib-

REPRESENTING JESUS IN THIS WORLD IS WORTH FIGHTING FOR

uting members of their communities and lifelong disciples of Christ. We will not give up believing that even the hardest heart can be impacted by the gospel and be turned around to become a follower of Christ. We believe this is our ultimate act of service: to fight for those who can't fight for themselves.

AN ARMY OF PLODDERS!

Christ-centred servant leaders stick it out with steel in their spines. They are gritty leaders who have learned to grow in faith, persevere through failure, and continue to fight the good fight. To some people this may sound glamorous, but sticking it out as a Christ-centred servant leader can also simply be a matter of resolving to make small steps of progress over the long haul.

William Carey is often called the father of modern missions. He was a missionary to India from 1793 to 1834. Among other things, he planted churches, started schools, campaigned for justice, translated scripture and started a Bible college. He knew the ups and downs of life through personal tragedies and discouragements on the mission field. But history records him as a great man of God

167

who had a massive kingdom impact. But what was his secret? In his own words, William Carey said:

'If one should think it worth his while to write my life, I will give you a criterion by which you may judge of its correctness. If he gives me credit for being a plodder, he will describe me justly. Anything beyond this will be too much. I can plod. I can persevere in any definite pursuit. To this I owe everything.'[85]

Carey knew what it was to stick it out. He had steel in his spine to plod – to persevere in the pursuit of his calling. Certainly, this was my experience during 2016. I needed to plod, to put one foot in front of the other, to continue doing simple everyday tasks, to persevere in order to care for myself and my children, and to trust that God would strengthen us to survive the tragedy and become stronger as a result of it.

Perhaps this is a goal for us all: to plod. Christ-centred servant leaders can persevere in any definite pursuit. To this we may owe everything, enabling us to become the kind of leaders that can bring genuine long-term transformation in the world. God can use faithful plodders who stick it out to the end.

There is nothing glamorous about grabbing a towel and kneeling to wash the muck and grime off people's feet. It requires the gritty resolve to stick it out – even if those same feet kick out at us, or run away and reject us. We don't become Christ-centred servant leaders because we will receive praise and rewards. No, we stick it out because our Master did so – and in him we see a model worth following, knowing that servant leaders have no guarantees of rewards, fame or fortune in this world.

But as we grab a towel and follow his example, we recognise that we are actually kneeling at his feet and worshipping him. As Christ-centred servant leaders we can stick it out with gritty determination because we know that it is him that we are ultimately serving.

'Whatever you do, work at it with all your heart, as working for the Lord, not for human masters, since you know that you will receive an inheritance from the Lord as a reward. It is the Lord Christ you are serving' (Col. 3:23-24).

PART THREE:
THE *GRAB A TOWEL* COMMITMENT

THE COMMITMENT

Having read *Grab A Towel,* are you prepared to commit to being a Christ-centred servant leader in the 21st century? Please read each statement overleaf carefully and then sign at the end as a covenant before God that you will seek to become the kind of leader that is worth following – the kind of leader that directs people to Jesus.

We are committed to being servant leaders who follow Christ and aspire to exemplify the following characteristics:

1. FOCUS ON CHARACTER

Christ-centred servant leaders increasingly exhibit the character of Christ.

It all starts with looking to Jesus. Christ-centred servant leaders love Jesus, spend time with him and seek that his character is formed within them. Jesus is their hero, their example and their best friend. Christ-centred servant leaders will continue to grow in Christ-like character and increasingly exhibit the characteristics of Christ throughout their lives.

Commitment statement: I am committed to becoming a Christ-centred servant leader who loves Jesus and desires for his character to be formed within me.

2. DEVELOP A PROPHETIC VISION

Christ-centred servant leaders have a gospel-focused vision that continues God's work on earth.

God is the author of mission and reveals his will and purposes to leaders in varied ways. Christ-centred servant leaders seek God for an image of the future and mobilise God's people towards a transformed future. The prophetic task of visionary leaders is to receive a specific vision from God, count the cost of obedience, and communicate clearly the vision to others.

Commitment statement: I am committed to becoming a Christ-centred servant leader who seeks God for a gospel-focused vision that continues his mission.

3. MAINTAIN FAITHFUL STEWARDSHIP

Christ-centred servant leaders are faithful stewards of the gospel in their generation.

Christ-centred servant leaders are custodians of the gospel in their generation and will be faithful stewards of the vision and calling God has placed upon their lives. They are responsible to leave a gospel legacy, facilitating the continued expansion of the kingdom into future generations until Christ shall return.

Commitment statement: I am committed to becoming a Christ-centred servant leader who will be a faithful steward of the calling to serve the gospel in my generation.

4. BECOME DEEP WELLS

Christ-centred servant leaders catalyse other leaders through growing in maturity.

Christ-centred servant leaders are men and women who are committed to keeping their spiritual wells full in order that they can have a deep impact in others and create a ripple effect of faithfulness to God that spans generations. Christ-centred servant leaders grow in maturity and depth as leaders throughout their lives to remain a deep well of resource to those they serve and to emerging leaders.

Commitment statement: I am committed to becoming a Christ-centred servant leader who will grow in spiritual maturity in order that I can be a deep well of resource to those I serve.

5. PUT PEOPLE FIRST

Christ-centred servant leaders put people before programmes, projects and profit.

Christ-centred servant leaders put other people first. They exist to prioritise people above their own interests and the interests of the organisation. They do this through fostering unity, teamwork and building trust.

Commitment statement: I am committed to becoming a Christ-centred servant leader who will put people before programmes, projects, and profit.

6. GIVE POWER AWAY

Christ-centred servant leaders empower others to fulfil their potential.

Christ-centred servant leaders give power away. They do not hold on to power but seek to empower others to fulfil their potential and even surpass them. This includes investing in emerging leaders whom they resource and relate to in an ongoing mentoring relationship.

Commitment statement: I am committed to becoming a Christ-centred servant leader who empowers others to fulfil their potential in faith, in life and in leadership.

7. LEAD WITH COMPASSION

Christ-centred servant leaders are motivated by compassionate love for others.

Christ-centred servant leaders are motivated by their compassion for other people. They seek to express love to those who are different to them, less privileged and most challenging to serve. Specifically, Christ-centred leaders focus on individuals, doing for one what they wish they could do for everyone.

Commitment statement: I am committed to becoming a Christ-centred servant leader who demonstrates compassionate love towards others, particularly those less privileged than myself.

8. HAVE STEEL IN YOUR SPINE

Christ-centred servant leaders have the steely resolve to persevere.

GRAB A TOWEL

Christ-centred servant leaders have the gritty resolve to persevere through all the challenges they face. They have steel in their spines which comes from recognising that God is sovereign and will work all things for good according to his perfect purposes. This enables them to grow in faith, endure through failings, and continue to fight the good fight.

Commitment statement: I am committed to becoming a Christ-centred servant leader who, through God's strength, will fight the good fight with steel in my spine, and endure to the end.

NAME: _____

SIGNED: _____

DATE: _____

THE *GRAB A TOWEL* WEBSITE

Grab A Towel and continue growing as a Christ-centred servant leader through visiting our website:

www.grabatowel.site

Join the conversation on Twitter and Facebook:

@GrabATowelBook

ACKNOWLEDGEMENTS

David Tucker (no relative) for helping me with the initial manuscript and ongoing encouragement with the project.

Dr Roger Tucker (my uncle) for reviewing (and challenging) the book from a theological perspective... I always appreciate your support and guidance.

Huge thanks and respect to all those at the Message family who haveve been part of the journey of writing this book over the past four years – particularly those who've been in my Leaders' Table groups: Tristan, Eppy, Cursurn, Luleka, Preston, Jessica, Alastair, Mthetheleli, Steve and Vuyo.

And to Christina: #ichooseyou.

NOTES

1   See more at www.lionsraw.org.

2   Umair Haque, 'How and why to be a leader (not a wannabe)' (https://hbr.org/2013/07/how-and-why-to-be-a-leader-not).

3   Ibid.

4   John Maxwell, *Leadership Gold: Lessons I've learned from a lifetime of leading* (Thomas Nelson, 2008), vii.

5   Taken from the foreword of my previous book, *The Pace Setter* (Message Books, 2014).

6   I recognise that not all the disciples would have been unschooled, and certainly the Apostle Paul was a well-educated and exceptionally gifted man. However, it is noteworthy that the phenomenal growth and impact of the New Testament church was catalysed by common people who had an extraordinary impact beyond their credentials, qualifications or social standing. God has often worked through 'unschooled and ordinary' people throughout church history as the catalyst for revival.

7   Address by Nelson Mandela during the 90th birthday celebration of Mr Walter Sisulu: http://www.mandela.gov.za/mandela_speeches/2002/020518_sisulu.htm

8   Nelson Mandela statement of defence at the Rivonia Trial, South Africa, April 20, 1964. See https://www.nelsonmandela.org/news/entry/i-am-prepared-to-die

9   Nelson Mandela's inaugural speech as President of South Africa, May 10, 1994.

10 Henry and Richard Blackaby, *Spiritual Leadership: Moving people on to God's agenda* (Broadman and Holman, 2001), 20.

11 Sen Sendjaya and James Sarros explain the difference in the two paradigms in their paper, *Servant Leadership: Its origin, development, and application* (2002): 'The servant leader operates on the assumption that "I am the leader, therefore I serve" rather than "I am the leader, therefore I lead." ...Servant leaders view themselves as the servant first, as distinguished from leaders first "who later serves out of promptings of conscience or in conformity with normative expectations."' (quoting Robert Greenleaf), pages 60 and 69.

12 Robert K Greenleaf, https://www.greenleaf.org/what-is-servant-leadership/

13 The Passion of the Christ, Dir. Mel Gibson, (Icon Productions, 2004).

14 Robert Clinton, *The Making of a Leader* (Navpress, 1988), 167.

15 Sendjaya and Sarros, *Servant Leadership: Its origin, development, and application*, 62.

16 A quick reading of the first few chapters of the Gospel of Mark, for example, demonstrates how approachable Jesus was. These action-packed verses show multiple interactions with individuals and crowds. Although Jesus was approachable, we also recognise that he did take time for retreat, prayer and reflection. He was able to be approachable because he maintained a vital relationship with his Father and was constantly led by the Holy Spirit (e.g. Mark 1:35-37).

17 Henry and Richard Blackaby, *Spiritual Leadership*, 105.

18 Article by John C. Maxwell at http://catalystconference.com/read/article-john-maxwell/

19 Robert Clinton, *The Making of a Leader*, 155.

20 JK Rowling, *Harry Potter and the Philosopher's Stone* (Bloomsbury, 1997), 230.

21 'Prayer is not so much about convincing God to do what we want God to do as it is about convincing ourselves to do what God wants us to do.' – Shane Claiborne, *Becoming the Answer to Our Prayers* (IVP, 2009), 11.

22 Many passages could be employed to further illuminate Christ's vision, but John 3:16-17; 6:38-39 and 14:6-7 clearly illustrate the future that Jesus envisaged.

23 'To the world, a good vision is an image of something that is both desirable and attainable. The difference between worldly visions and God-given visions is that God-given visions are always impossible to achieve without God. In this regard, Christian leaders have a tremendous advantage over secular leaders. People want to be a part of something significant. People want their lives to make a difference in their world. People want to be a part of something God is doing. If it is clear that God has made a promise to a group of people, there should be little difficulty in enlisting the support of group members.' Henry and Richard Blackaby, *Spiritual Leadership*, 74.

24 See Bill Hybels, *Holy Discontent* (Zondervan, 2007).

25 'A clear vision provides a compelling picture of the future that enables us to say, 'We know our destination. Nothing will lure us off the path from here to there. We will not be distracted.' Bill Hybels, *Courageous Vision* (Zondervan, 2009), 48.

26 'Planning that arises from and is the product of prayer is far superior to planning that is merely "backed by" prayer. The plan that is God's plan, revealed by him to those who wait on him, is a plan that cannot fail. Real efficiency comes from waiting on God.' John White, *Excellence in Leadership* (IVP, 1986), 36.

27 'Waiting on God does not mean that detailed information and research are unnecessary. Nehemiah will need to find out for himself – another basic principle in promoting efficiency... we are irresponsible when we do not find out for ourselves... To walk by faith means that knowing the problems, we look to God for solutions.' John White, *Excellence in Leadership*, 38.

28 Lon Fendall, *To Live Free: Experiencing the Man, the Mission, and the Legacy* (Barbour Publishing, 2007), 111.

29 Henry and Richard Blackaby, *Spiritual Leadership*, 75.

30 Angus Buchan, Facebook post, April 16, 2013.

31 Downton Abbey, Series 1, episode 4, by Julian Fellowes and Shelagh Stephenson (Carnival Film and Television, 2010).

32 Ibid.

33 Phrase taken from the online resource Bible Study Tools, https://www.biblestudytools.com/dictionary/steward/

34 Albert Mohler, 'Leadership as Stewardship', http://www.albertmohler.com/2013/04/08/leadership-as-stewardship-part-one/

35 Watchman Nee, *Sit, Walk, Stand* (Victory Press, 1970), 56.

36 R K Hughes, *Living on the Cutting Edge* (Crossway Books, 1987), 30.

37 Wooden in Brian Biro, *Beyond Success: The 15 secrets to effective leadership and life based on legendary coach John Wooden's pyramid of success* (Berkley Publishing Group, 1977) :xvii.

38 Peter Williams puts it like this: 'Ministry is hard, painstaking work, and God requires his servants, in the first instance, not to be 'successful', but to be faithful. The success or otherwise can be safely left in his hands.' Peter Williams, *Opening up 2 Timothy* (Day One Publications, 2007), 97.

39 John Ashmen, *Invisible Neighbours* (Cross Section, 2011), 38.

40 John D H Greenway, *The Leaders' Map* (Kindle edition, 2013) location 868.

41 Robert Clinton, *The Making of a Leader*, 199.

42 AW Tozer, *The Root of the Righteous* (OM Publishing, 1955), 72.

43 Ibid., 74.

44 Jim Collins, *Great By Choice* (HarperCollins, 2011), 21.

45 Robert Clinton, *The Making of a Leader*, 89

46 Brian Biro, *Beyond Success*, 273.

47 Charles Haddon Spurgeon, *Sermons, Vol. 15:1869*, 134.

NOTES

48 Brian Biro, *Beyond Success*, 197.

49 Liquorice Allsorts: just in case you've never eaten them... a childhood favourite sweet of mine that my kids and I love to eat on long hikes. Each pack contains an assortment of sweets, each equally delicious and addictive!

50 Rinehart says, 'If the example of the Trinity were better reflected in our practices of spiritual leadership, we would see a blessed difference in the way we operate with each other. Greater unity of heart would prevail, and leadership would manifest itself in others-oriented acts of service. Our prevailing leadership style would be based on the model of servanthood, with the final focus resting on the example of our triune God.' Stacy Rinehart, *Upside Down* (Navpress, 1998), 90.

51 John Maxwell, http://www.johnmaxwell.com/blog/one-is-too-small-a-number

52 A term coined by Stacy Rinehart in *Upside Down*, 93.

53 Ibid.

54 Ibid.

55 Alan J Roxburgh and Fred Romanuk, *The Missional Leader* (Jossey-Bass, 2006), 127.

56 I acknowledge the influence of Steven Covey, *The 7 Habits of Highly Effective People* (Simon and Schuster, 2004), in these elements that help build trust. Covey writes, 'Trust is the highest form of human motivation. It brings out the very best in people. But it takes time and patience, and it doesn't preclude the necessity to train and develop people so that their competency can rise to the level of that trust', 178.

57 Angus Buchan, *Living a Mighty Faith* (Thomas Nelson, 2016), 167.

58 Bill Thrall, Bruce McNicol, Ken McElrath, *The Ascent of a Leader* (Jossey-Bass, 1999), 83.

59 Robert Lupton, *Toxic Charity* (Harper Collins, 2011), 129.

60 With thanks to David Tucker.

61 Kent Hunter. *Burn On or Burn Out: Thriving in Kingdom Culture* (www.churchdoctor.org, 2017), 4.

62 Corbett and Fikkert, *When Helping Hurts* (Moody, 2012), 109. Also, Tony Campolo and Shane Claiborne conclude the following: 'One of the things I discovered in the red letters of the Bible is that Jesus doesn't do for us what we can do for ourselves. Instead he says, "The work that I do, you shall do. And you will do even greater works than I have done because I am empowering you to do it." That emphasis, the empowerment of people, should become the new direction of missionary work because the old ways, in so many instances, have proven to be counterproductive.' Shane Claiborne and Tony Campolo, *Red Letter Christianity* (Hodder and Stoughton), 242.

63 My previous book, *The Pace Setter*, looks more thoroughly at the subject of mentoring emerging leaders. This section summarises a small portion of the material in that book.

64 Kent Hunter and Tracee Swankee, *Who Broke my Church?: 7 proven strategies for renewal and revival* (FaithWords, 2017), 58.

65 I am indebted to Gareth Lloyd-Jones for these four Rs.

66 Brian Biro, *Beyond Success*, 123.

67 As quoted in Edward Le Joly and Jaya Chaliha, *Mother Teresa's Reaching Out In Love: Stories told by Mother Teresa* (Barnes & Noble, 2002), 122

68 Brennan Manning, *The Ragamuffin Gospel* (Authentic Lifestyle, 2007), 152.

69 Martin Luther King Jr, 'A time to break silence,' speech given at Riverside Church, NY, 4 April 1967. http://www.americanrhetoric.com/speeches/mlkatimetobreaksilence.htm

70 Amplified Bible (AMP) Copyright © 2015 by The Lockman Foundation.

71 Gregory Boyle, *Tattoos on the Heart* (Simon and Schuster, 2010), 67.

72 Ibid., 72.

73 Father Boyle says, 'The strategy of Jesus is not centred in taking the right stand on issues, but rather in standing in the right place - with the outcast and those relegated to the margins.' Ibid., 72.

74 Ibid., 188.

75 Joel Manby, *Love Works: Seven timeless principles for effective leaders* (Zondervan, 2012) 102.

76 See www.joineden.org. The Message has launched more than 50 such teams around the world.

77 'Getting things done quickly is simply not what development is all about! Development is a lifelong process, not a two-week product.' Steven Corbett and Brian Fikkert, *When Helping Hurts*, 157.

78 This could not be better expressed than in the words of John in his first letter: 'Dear friends, let us love one another...' (1 John 1:7-12)

79 Traditionally it has been told that William Booth included these words at his final sermon at the Royal Albert Hall, 19 May 1912. However it is probable it's from an earlier period. See discussion on when Booth first spoke these words in John G. Merritt and Allen Satterlee, *Historical Dictionary of the Salvation Army* (Rowman and Littlefied, 2017), 237.

80 Quoted by Warren Wiersbe, *Be Comforted* (David Cook, 1992), 133.

81 Bill Hybels speaking at the Global Leadership Summit 2015.

82 Jim Collins, *Great by Choice*, 182.

83 Dan Palotta, The way we think about charity is dead wrong. TED Talk 2013, https://www.ted.com/talks/dan_pallotta_the_way_we_think_about_charity_is_dead_wrong/transcript

84 Henry and Richard Blackaby, *Spiritual Leadership*, 191. Henry Cloud concurs, 'The best performers know how to fail well. They see it, accept it, and move on. They do not keep beating the dead horse, or worse, riding the one with the broken leg. They can call it quits, wave the white flag, and go forward.' Henry Cloud, *Necessary Endings* (HarperCollins, 2010), 50.

85 Warren Wiersbe, *Be Comforted*, 133.

SUPPORT MESSAGE SOUTH AFRICA

The Message Trust South Africa shares the good news of the Christian message to youth at risk across Cape Town. We believe that young people from difficult backgrounds can turn their lives around and become transformational leaders in society. Our task is to create an environment for 'urban heroes' to flourish in faith and life. We summarise what we do as follows:

1. **Identify.** We go where others may be too scared to go... to tough neighbourhoods and prisons in order to identify young people with potential and share the Christian message of hope with them.
2. **Platform.** Our various programmes provide a platform for young people who want to leave the gangs/prison and rebuild their lives to become productive members of society. Our programmes are in tough communities, prison, schools and through micro-business.
3. **Mission.** Ultimately we want the young people we reach to recognise that they themselves can be used by God to make a difference in the world – that they can get on mission and start a ripple effect of transformation. We want to contribute to a new story in South Africa... one that breaks down stigma and barriers.

Ultimately we believe the church can make a difference in society and we want to equip the church to effectively reach young people. We believe young people are looking for a cause... and we want to get young people on mission to make South Africa a better place for everyone.

PLEASE CONSIDER SUPPORTING OUR WORK IN PRAYER AND FINANCIALLY.

SEE MESSAGE.ORG.ZA FOR MORE INFORMATION.